T0064230

Gender Gamut

Selected Essays About Women

Gender Gamut

Selected Essays About Women

Syeda Afshana

PARTRIDGE
A Penguin Random House Company

Copyright © 2015 by Syeda Afshana.

ISBN: Softcover   978-1-4828-5841-9
             eBook   978-1-4828-5840-2

All rights reserved. No part of this book may be used or reproduced by any means, graphic, electronic, or mechanical, including photocopying, recording, taping or by any information storage retrieval system without the written permission of the author except in the case of brief quotations embodied in critical articles and reviews.

Because of the dynamic nature of the Internet, any web addresses or links contained in this book may have changed since publication and may no longer be valid. The views expressed in this work are solely those of the author and do not necessarily reflect the views of the publisher, and the publisher hereby disclaims any responsibility for them.

Print information available on the last page.

To order additional copies of this book, contact
Partridge India
000 800 10062 62
orders.india@partridgepublishing.com

www.partridgepublishing.com/india

❧

For
my little angels
Abdullah and Ausaf

❧

Contents

Woman: God's second mistake? 1
Woman: A colourful contradiction................................. 4
Woman: Martyr of Chick Lit.. 7
Woman: The Muse Incarnate......................................11
Woman, angel, mother...15
Women: Between Extremities 18
Moolah Not Morality 23
Failed Goddesses... 27
Between within & without... 32
Gender Gamut.. 36
She shouldn't be born 40
India's Shame 43
Generational Saga 47
The Lonely Dolls 50
A Creative Symphony... 54
We: the Change Agent 58
Let her live 61
Characters Cry 66
Beyond barbarity... 69
Crime against women 72
She's Mouj.. 76
Lala Ded : Communicator Par Excellence?.....................81
The Life Pullers.. 86
White House Epics 90
IB-intellectuals.. 95
False theme song 98

She is on street 101

Breathing in turmoil 104

Shame on us!..107

Allama Iqbal's Feminism...............................110

The Finest Relation.......................................114

Women of Piety 117

Real Success 121

Past has to pass...125

Home, a small magic world......................... 128

Woman: God's second mistake?

Friedrich Nietzsche, a German philosopher, who regarded 'thirst for power' as the sole driving force of all human actions, has many a one-liners to his credit. 'Woman was God's second mistake', he declared. Unmindful of the reactionary scathing criticism and shrill abuses he invited for himself, especially from the ever-irritable feminist brigade.

The fact and belief that God never ever commits a mistake, brings Nietzsche's proclamation dashingly down into the dust bin of nonsense. Whatever Almighty God has created is beautiful and useful. His creative powers are fabulous, beyond the purlieus of any kind of fallacy. God created Adam and Eve – both the remarkable assets for humanity. The fault never lies with the Creator—the only Infallible. It's rather always with the 'created' who deviate from the prescribed natural laws of living. And it surely goes without saying that woman, the best creation of God, has done the same, bringing a bad name to her existence.

Serving as a waitress in a café, clerk in offices, sales girl, air hostess, massage hand and performing any dirty or white collar job, she has in a way become instrumental in vandalizing the essence of womanhood. And ironically, she has started becoming absolutely desensitized in this regard and views such revolting displays of degradation as 'progress' and worthy of emulation! Reeling under the impact of onslaught from Western libertinism, she has banished all some critical concepts of womanhood from her mind and heart. The libertine culture of the West with its total advocacy of sexual mingling has influenced her thought power and disabled her to see beyond the materialistic cult. West has diligently pursued the task of brainwashing and as such gentleness and humility are no longer now the attributes of woman of East. Thanks to the mundane education and salacious media, and over-all social milieu that's favourably shaping up the ground for all this.

Today, it is too vivid that a divergent view or ideology has emerged in opposition to unanimously mankind held view regarding the ruinous consequences of sexual liberalism, which by now has culminated in the calamity of spiritual retrogression. A stage where demarcation of good and bad vanishes, and individuals of a society or a nation are driven into the amphitheatres of immoderately high and mighty desires. Woman, in this whole background, cannot be exonerated just as a victim of circumstances. Her obsession to be like a man paves the way of her downfall, and when she falls, she falls not alone but drags with herself man also.

While commenting on such an obsessive attitude of the woman, which she manifests in different forms, Jennifer Coates in '*Women, Men and Language*' writes, "They perceive themselves as belonging to an inferior group (women) and attempt to assimilate the values of the superior group (men). They adopt what they perceive to be male values". There is no denying the fact that at any stage of life every woman perforce suffers from a sort of inferiority complex, and just out of sheer egoism she wants to suppress it somehow. And in doing so, she adopts the male values out and out. From air force to truck driving, she makes her presence felt and stakes the claim that she can stand as tall as the man. This is what the feminist brigade likes to call as her 'heroism' and has been elevated to what is known as the 'sexual revolution' which, we are told, is the price of 'modernity.'

The woman of East has, unfortunately, without any reservations purchased this 'modernity' for herself, and she is paying a huge price. It is, of course, not a best buy. For what use the 'freedom' which costs you your essence dearly, which robs you of your individuality, and which snatches away all your tranquillity and solace?

The much-hyped 'emancipation' has shown woman nothing but the tragedy of being a weaker sex in a greedy media-induced world where she gets reduced to an image of cultural consumption. Such 'emancipation' has, in reality, denied her real autonomy and killed her spirituality. Her life has turned into nothing but a master narrative; everyone seeks to consume it. Beneath the flimsiness and hollowness of what she is today, there is a simmering discontent, a painful realization of what she is not. Bold-eyed, her 'freedom' is provocative and her learning inadequate to bear the charge of motherhood. A riot in her glance, she is no more than a skeleton-figured bamboo, whose thoughts are resplendent with nothing but the 'Western light'. To quote Allama Iqbal:

> *On the dusk and evening of her days,*
> *not one star shines.*
> *Her sacred charms are*
> *all unloosed and spilled.*
> *Inwardly, no woman she!*

Woman: A colourful contradiction

People of different idiosyncrasies have described woman differently. From ballads to odes, plays to novels, she has been portrayed in various roles variably. Whether it is Maxim Gorky's heroine Nilovna, Bathsheba of Thomas Hardy, Lady Macbeth of Shakespeare or Keat's La Belle Della Sans Merci—no holds have been barred by whimsical wordsmiths to highlight, delight, slight and blight woman!

Fiction apart, in factuality woman is much more than a bundle of traditional fables and over killed clichés. She is a special creation of Almighty with an extra special purpose of life, contrary to what drowsy poets and demented feminist writers have been aligning to her. She is the perfect workmanship of God; the true glory of Angels; the rare miracle of Earth; and the sole wonder of the World. Mankind is indebted to her: first for life itself and then for making it worth having. Aptly said—

Wajood-i-Zan Say Hai
Tasweerey Kainaat Main Rang....

Down the memory lane, one can trace out her journey, when not long ago in the West she was tied up to a horse and carried through the streets. Those were the times when Christianity had declared her as *Devil Incarnate* and the church authorities were seriously discussing if she had a soul at all. She wasn't any better in the East where she was burnt alive with her dead husband. However, that was the ephemeral dark period in the history of her existence. Perhaps. Since then she has been going 'up and up and on the ladder of emancipation'.

Initially she had individual champions speaking for her. John Stuwart Mill and Mary Wollstonecraft, for instance. Today she has whole organizations working for her 'cause' such as the Women's Lib or the United Nations and has the entire media in her support. In addition to much-talked international conferences every year, March 8 is celebrated as International Women's Day for her betterment. Indeed, it appears as an enviable privilege for the Eve of today, who is always lamenting and clamouring for her 'rights'. She barely misses any opportunity to present herself as the most 'oppressed and deprived'. Women's Day, in such context, fortuitously comes in handy for her to sell hogwash slogans and mottos of 'rebellion' against all. Rallies, seminars and debates mark the day which she brags wholly as hers. And seemingly at odds with the whole world, she leaves no stone unturned to hold all and sundry responsible for her present 'plight'.

Woman's at best a contradiction still – this is what Alexander Pope opines in his moral essays. Does not his assessment about woman sound solid and relevant? It's really damn difficult to suggest 'woman's nature' in abstraction. In the contemporary world, there are any numbers of stereotype images ranging from King Lear's wife (Schemer) to Portia (dispenser of justice) in Shakespeare's plays to Hardy's women like Bathsheba wherein Hardy expresses a certain cynicism with regard to their conduct to the Victorian prudishness.

Once one descends into history to look for the essence of woman, it becomes a strenuous and an uncertain exercise, for woman has always lived by her heart and not head. One fails to understand, even today, the intricate psychology of woman, especially that of the East. On one hand, she is out and out intoxicated with the concept of liberalism, and contrarily she blames others for the deplorable fall-out of such intoxication. How crazy!

In fact, the problem with her is that she isn't able to identify and sense the consequences of rubbing shoulders with men in almost every field. To satisfy her false ego, she cares a tinker's damn for her identity. In the pursuit of so-called emancipation and freedom, she is, in fact, seeking slavery to world of hypocrite and lustful men. Hardly does she realize that true freedom is in refusal to sell one self and true solace in recognizing the poverty of her material affluence.

No doubt, today's woman breathes and lives amidst the concept of feminism. 'Don't make coffee, make policy'— such slogans are continuously being injected into her mind. She is being bombarded with 'Hate-Man-Hate-Mankind' type of rabid feminism.

However, to sustain the aura of her individuality, and above all, the essence of her womanhood, her feminism should be of different kind, beyond the comprehension of the high academic culture of so-called feminism. Because she must know that she is neither competing with men nor trying to show them down. She should simply realize and value what she has been gifted with: the infinite power of life-affirming love and maternity. Her language should not be the language of separation, narcissism and competition; it should be the language of love, patience and generosity.

So, let her formulate good policies. Without forgetting how to prepare a cup of coffee as well! Let life and its pristine melody touch her. All along the years, and not just on the eve of March 8.

Woman: Martyr of Chick Lit

They say, there are two tests of the philosophy of life. That is, the test of truth and the test of morality. Truth in fiction means something else while the truth in works of science has a different meaning. When Plato said that all imaginative literature is "false" because it does not reproduce the actual facts of life, he was perhaps too judgmental. Aristotle pointed out the basic fallacy in Plato's view. He maintained that there exists in all great works of imagination a "poetic truth" which is much more comprehensive than mere literal fidelity to the facts in the work of a historian. The historian is bound to things which have actually taken place, whilst the creative artist is limited only by what Aristotle called 'ideal probability'. In the former, truth means fidelity to what was or is; in the latter, truth implies fidelity to what may be.

Thus, it could be argued that the truth of literature is fidelity to the 'making of utopias'—where anything goes as concocted ambiguities are likely to remain unresolved and confounded as ever. Almost all eminent writers, especially those belonging to the West, have tread the same path. In the process, 'magnificent' literary treatises passed down have often used woman as a spicy condiment, eventually devaluing and debasing her natural role, even if unintentionally.

From Shakespeare's plays, wherein women have been rendered ineluctable paradoxes, to nearer home Arundhati

Roy's GOST heroine, who ultimately pays the unchaste 'cost of living'—Wordsmiths have always muffled women with their literary tantrums. It's widely accepted that the Bard-of-Avon broke away from the stereotyped morality plays. He destroyed the reigning, stultifying over-simplifications of Elizabethan drama. He is critiqued as portraying 'heroes with flaws and un-heroic impulses, and heroines whose chastity was at war with their carnality'. However, in every feminine character of his, there seems a criss-cross of identities, a colour of conundrums. In *Antony and Cleopatra,* the heroine has been declared as a 'courtesan of genius' who becomes almost a tragic figure and 'a martyr to the cause of love'. But the whole saga is highly conjectural in the annals of history. That Greek historians gave Cleopatra the title of *Meriochane,* meaning a woman who can devour ten thousand men, outrightly nullifies her so-called martyrdom for the sake of love. The way Cleopatra dramatically presented herself to Julius Caesar of Rome, and after his assassination drew Mark Antony in to her dragnet, is by far the most disgraceful chapter of any woman-ruler in the world. But eulogy showered on her by Shakespeare flunks out his literal sensibility vis-à-vis woman.

Strangely enough, there is an antithesis of vampy Cleopatra in another play *Macbeth*—a riveting tale about two murderers, husband and wife, locked in their evil and intertwining guilt. Lady Macbeth is a woman who ruthlessly re-asserts herself only to perish at the hands of nemesis. Her last appearance speaks the futility of her bloody career—wringing hands smeared in blood, trying even in her sleep to alleviate her guilt: *'Here's the smell of blood still. All the perfumes of Arabia will not sweeten this little hand'*. The real femme-fatale, Lady Macbeth, characterized yet another wildly imaginative wantonness of Shakespeare. Incidentally, an enormous academic speculation of his being a bi-sexual is still revolving, as also vindicated by such overtones even in his love stories like *Romeo and Juliet* and *Othello*.

There are numerous instances when in the name of creativity, the image of woman was dipped into loathing world of promiscuity, only to add flavour to the filthy pot-pourri of perverted minds. D.H. Lawrence's *Lady Chatterley's Lover,* first published in 1928, was immediately banned because of the outrageously obscene depiction of the relationship between the heroine Connie and her husband's gamekeeper, Oliver Mellor. Lawrence's work marked a watershed in history by socially 'legitimizing' licentiousness. With gradual change of moral climate, permission was given to republish it in 1959. Deeply 'inspired' by this bodice ripper, a whole spate of similar literature followed. The people with 'creative genius' set the ball rolling for raking up dirt, with woman as the cynosure of their new-found literary lunacy. Some of them even got rewarded!

Interestingly, there is a striking similarity in the affair between Ammu and Velutha in *The God of Small Things* (GOST) with the one depicted by Lawrence. The kind of relationship that developed between the two has the primeval quality of the Connie-Mellors affairs in *Lady Chatterley*. In fact, to make gravy *(Chutney– fiction)* saucer, Arundhati has introduced all necessary ingredients in the GOST– onanism, homosexuality, fornication, adultery and what not.

Be it Chutney-fiction, Chick-Lit or for that matter any poetic and literary works going under the genre of romanticism, etc., the fact remains that woman enjoys a central character. Rather, she is the favourite whipping horse of the lickerish masters of these forms of literature all over the world. She adds 'spice' to otherwise 'bland' world of poets, 'glitter' to the dull and drab literary monsters—that have tags of 'classics' and other things attached. In fact, woman fits in to any scheme to make conspicuous the individuals in the guise of literature, poetry *et al.* She supposedly adores the world of literati. The harsh realities, however, is that her eternal deprecation may have earned accolades for many who had lived in obscurity and were paupers forsaken by their own people. The million dollar question is what has woman earned in exchange by perpetual recycling at this painfully obnoxious yet comforting sacrificial altar perpetuated by Lotharios of literature.

Is she happy being a scapegoat?

Woman: The Muse Incarnate

Someone has well said: "There is no Truth, only there are truths." The truths are many, and many are their meanings. Life is just a one truth, with a multi-dimensional luminosity. Contemplation or thinking is simply a small part of this whole. According to a Yale University scientist, David Gelernter, "all human beings slide along a spectrum of thought processes on an average day. This begins with 'high-focus' thinking where we sandwich many memories and pieces of know ledge, and quickly extract the thing they all have in common".

It is not so much creative ability as assimilative expertise aiding swift decisions and quick action. Sliding along the spectrum is 'low-focus', where we become less good at homing in on details, but our memories are more vivid, concrete and detailed. As per Gelernter, it is when people are in 'middle-focus' that they are at their most creative. This is because the mind is free from both concerns and un-reasonable emotions. In 'middle-focus', people make unusual connections: Newton and the apple; Archimedes and the bath tub; Kekule and the two snakes; Wordsworth and leech gatherer; Ghalib and *Bazichae atfaal* (children's plaything); and so on. This mode provides person the right insight into things that are already in high-focus. From literary point of view, it involves imagination and a penchant for novelty. Poets and writers have always produced their best in 'middle-focus': The state of mind where living in the midst of storms, with effort and fortitude, they arrive at a mode of acceptance and understanding of life with a creative genius.

The role of women, in this regard, has been debatable. Leaving out the element of 'unusually', they have created various masterpieces—both imaginative and pragmatic. In fact, it is presumed that women have the capability of mastering the tradition of creative writing a bit better, since they often write diaries and read more fiction. The road has already been traversed many years ago by Fanny Burney, Aphra Behn, Harriet Martineau, George Eliot, Jane Austen, Virginia Woolf, Emily Bronte, Ayn Rand and many other famous women writers. Writing has been a very reputable and harmless occupation for women. It is a still stranger thing that there is nothing so delightful in the world as telling stories. In *Professions for Women,* an enigmatic piece by Virginia Woolf, she delineates a picture of young girl struggling to write down a few lines – "There is a girl sitting with a pen in her hand, which for minutes, and indeed for hours, she never dips into the inkpot. Like a fisherman, she was sunk in dreams on the verge of a deep lake with a rod held out over the water. She was letting her imagination sweep unchecked round every rock and cranny of the world that lies submerged in the depths of unconscious being. Now came the experience, the experience that I believe to be far commoner with women writers than with men. The line raced through the girl's fingers. Her imagination had rushed away. It had sought the pools, the depths, the dark places where the largest fish slumber. And then there was a smash. There was an explosion. The imagination had dashed itself against something hard. To speak without figure, the girl had thought of something that was unfitting for her to say. The consciousness of what men will say of a woman who speaks truth had roused her from her artist's state of unconsciousness. She could write no more. Her imagination could work no longer. This I believe to be a very common experience with women writers—they are impeded by the extreme conventionality."

It is a conundrum as what really does the 'conventionalism' connote. It's a relative concept for no woman writer has her identity outside the culture she is born or brought up. History, heritage, ancestry etc., all combine to condition the writer's imagination. She carries in her work the genes of her race, and the gist of its intellectual and moral life. These strains, therefore, are a fact of her world-view and are impregnable enough to be violated by her artistic imagination. Whatever her shared perception and experience, woman as a writer has always displayed a *carte blanche,* having no ghosts to fight and no rocks to dash down. Virginia Woolf's premise, as such, can either be a weak generalization or simply a self-begotten vague hypothesis.

Contrarily, Jane Austen has been a writer with a difference. She has remained unsurpassed in her artistic mastery in fiction. Her works are the products of her profound vision of life. It is a vision so constantly held and consistently presented that some say if she had been born a man then, or a woman in this more indulgent age, it might almost have been called *thought.* Jane Austen had a streak of genius that gave her the uncanny insight into the minds and motives of human beings, and the power to transfer it to paper which immortalized her name quite differently in the annals of literature. Confronted with nothing like 'conventional syndrome', she spoke her mind as she wanted. While Wordsworth, Shelly and Keats were emphasizing the supremacy of the heart, Jane Austen followed a differently indigenous tradition. She stoutly opposed an uninhibited and crude display of emotions advocated by her great contemporaries, who incidentally happened to be men. This mindset of hers finds powerful expression in her novel *Sense and Sensibility*. Writing with a clear purpose and perfect consciousness of what she was doing, Jane unlike many others serenaded her imagination into arbors of sunshine instead of drowning it into sabled sentimentalism.

Whether or not women are more creative than men and whether qualitatively their literary endeavours are better, could be debated endlessly. All art forms, literature being one among them, irrespective of their origin can achieve excellence only until they reflect the reality with minimal distortion. Real time portrayal of life's complexities, tragedies, ecstasies and various situations constitute the best of literature in any language, location, at any point of history.

Ironically, its perhaps women writers who have also marked watershed in the history of literature by putting up 'works' that are whirlpools of confusing and ambiguous ideals, erratic behaviours, unnatural matrix of strange coincidences, stretched beyond imagination and what not.

Nevertheless, it is not surprising to expect the best from women as writers for they possess that *womanly touch* that can bring alive on those lifeless pages the sheen of life, its magnificence, the loveliness as well as its ugly side. The despair and the hope; the pain and the pleasure; the sweet and the sour; the tear and the joy—so much apart, yet always side by side.

Woman, angel, mother

I wondered why a caller asked the question that was not related to the topic under discussion. While rushing towards the workplace during morning hours, I was listening to a phone-in radio program hosted by a certain *Maulana* on the topic of *Zakat*.

A frail elderly woman, who had asked for a lift earlier, was also listening to the program while traveling with me. "*Maulana sahib* should take his problem seriously and help him out. In fact, this problem is becoming grave and needs to be addressed," she reacted suddenly.

The caller had asked, "What should I do when my mother and my wife have no common platform of understanding? The atmosphere in our home is tense. I have all respect for my parents but I love my wife as well."

There was nothing surprising in this question, as it seemed a relatively familiar debate, often talked about. However, the caller's desperation was something disquieting. I was trying to empathize with the poor fellow. Before I could, actually, the woman beside me spouted forth, "Do you know what is the real blessing from Allah and a valueless jewel for a woman?" I was caught up in a reverie for the right answer, and before I could say something she said, "A loving and a caring husband." I was a bit stunned to hear wisdom from her. Her demeanor gave no reflection of her mind. A modest woman, probably in her sixties, seemed a plain

Jane. Unpretentiously, she questioned again-"In return what should wife do to show her gratitude to Allah for blessing her with a wonderful husband?" While I was amazingly looking towards her, she voiced strongly, "She should show gratitude to her husband's parents for educating him about the dealings of life. Today, if he is loving and affectionate towards her wife, it is actually the outcome of the upbringing and education that has been imparted to him by his parents. He might have been fashioned and brought to this shape after endless sacrifices of his parents. That is why she should help her husband to be closer to Allah by reminding him to be obedient and polite to his parents, and same applies for the husband as well."

After a brief pause, she stared me with piercing eyes. I got a bit nervy. Then abruptly, she said in a polite tone, "There should be no other satisfaction and tranquility for a wife than seeing her husband fulfilling the commandments of Allah. Just selflessly, only for the sake of Allah, without expecting anything in return in this world". I nodded my head and tried to say something. But she didn't allow any breathing space and rapidly said, "Do you know that taking care of parents is one of the commandments as Allah has placed parents second to Him in holy Quran?" I again nodded my head. This time very fast. But she proved faster and continued, "Don't say a word of contempt to your parents—Allah says. When one's parents get into the old age, they might exhibit certain tantrums and may display changes in their behavior due to age related changes. Their dealings may be annoying for their children. Nevertheless, in no case should their children deal with them harshly or just abandon them."

After this, she was all at once quiet. She heaved a sigh, peeped out from the window glass, and turned her head away. An unpredictable but somber silence lasted for a few minutes. I attempted to break the ice by saying without any thought, "Today's mother-in-law has been yesterday's wife. She has been a daughter as well. What is her responsibility in all this?

She did not answer for a while. I thought I posed a wrong query to a right person. However, without turning towards me, she replied-"Being the elder of home, she has a lot of experience with her. Mother-in-law is ought to have excelled in patience and perseverance while playing the role of a daughter, then a wife, later a mother and now a mother-in-law. She is expected to have risen above many small things than being unforgiving, intolerant, and hard-hearted."

Before she could again carry on relentlessly, she sharply sensed her destination and said, "Please stop, stop. I will get down here." She stepped down in haste and faded out from sight.

Did I see this face for the first time or it seemed too familiar?....I was in a dilemma. Perhaps rethinking about an angel of my childhood storybooks, etched in my mind, who would come in different forms to convey the message of Almighty. The old woman did not look angelic. But her words were so. Else she echoed like a motherly figure, refreshing what conventional mother keeps telling her daughter as she grows up for leaving her home and her parents for good. Mother keeps reminding about seraphic traits of exemplary sacrifice and patience. She can ignore the things and situations that may hurt or disappoint her as long as her husband respects and loves her.

An ordinary woman, a haunting angel, a loving mother, or a seraphic character—perhaps, it does not matter who is the speaker. What matters is the message. And what means is the role.

Women: Between Extremities

Bertrand Russell once remarked that Aristotle was highly ignorant, if not irrational, about women. While proving the 'inferiority' of women, Aristotle had stated that women have fewer teeth than men. Russell snuffed out the senseless logic saying: "Although Aristotle was twice married, it never occurred to him to verify this statement by examining his wives' mouths" (*Impact of Science on Society, p-17*).

It's obvious that even great thinkers bungle at the issue of woman. Even as she always occupies the centre-stage of discourses and confabs, her existence is proportionately turning more complex and contrapositive to a naturally simple one. Dogmatic absurdity apart, her feminine essence is torn asunder by baseless propaganda. And if she happens to be the adherent of Islamic faith, then malicious storm is sure to toss her over.

In a recent on-line *New York Times* article about American Muslim women, the writer paints a cynical picture citing the example of one Rose Hamid. The intro of article pronounces: "Rose Hamid is as American as they come. She drives a Ford station wagon, leads a local Girl Scout troupe, shops at the Gap and just attended her 20-year high school reunion."

From this brief description of Rose, readers may have formed a particular picture of her in their minds. If they were told, however, that Rose Hamid wears a headscarf in keeping with her Muslim faith, that picture might take a drastic turn. Is she Muslim? The question will surely pop up. Then the images of suppressed, meek, black-enshrouded women submitting to the demands of their 'dominating husbands' will race through the minds of many western readers. Since Rose Hamid is a Muslim woman, it is difficult not to have some pre-conceived notions about her. And why not, Muslim women in the West have always been clumped in to one large group and viewed as homogenous clone of one another, whilst their Jewish and Christian counterparts are rarely ever typecast in this way.

Perhaps due to immensely biased media interpretations, many people don't realize that there is large variety of Muslim women around the world, from areas such as the Middle East, South Asia, South East Asia, Yugoslavia, Northern Africa, and the southern parts of erstwhile USSR, just as there are Christian and Jewish women in various countries. For instance, one probably wouldn't classify a Mexican woman with a French woman, though both may be Roman Catholics and share the same beliefs. In the same way, American Muslim women are different from their Pakistani counterparts, who are different from those in Saudi Arabia. In these countries, women are accorded different rights and privileges because of the social, economic, cultural and governmental set-ups of the area. Many American Muslim women are discriminated against because they cover their heads; Pakistani women have political rights but are often exploited; Saudi Women have no public role, yet they are the most secure and protected. The negative stereotypes of Muslim women probably arise from this varying treatment of women. This comes handy for the Western media, whose favorite pastime is to latch on to a few examples of illogical and aberrant behaviour and brand Islam as an "orthodox" religion, especially in its treatment of women.

Often, the western media blatantly portray the Muslim decency as a suppressing factor in a woman's life. Every Muslim woman is required to don modest attire, and this *per se* is not a means of controlling a woman's sexuality or suppressing her. Dressing modestly elevates a woman from being seen as a mere sex symbol to a unique and magnificent entity – position reserved for her only. It is one of the great ironies of present world that the very same headscarf revered as a sign of holiness when worn for the purpose of showing the authority of man by Catholic Nuns, is revile as a sign of 'orthodoxy' when worn for the purpose of modesty by Muslim women. Doublespeak dominates. The example of heated conflict over Muslim dress that became an intense emotional issue of the 1994 academic year in France is worth mentioning. The Principal of a school in Creil refused to let three Muslim girls wear the headscarf to school. The French Education Minister banished 'ostentatious' religious symbols in schools. Interestingly, crucifixes and Star of David were not considered as ostentatious!!!

There is no denying that with the progression of time, the genuine rights of Muslim women have fizzled out. The deviation from Islam can be noticed by evaluating the rights that women possess in different countries across the world. America, thought not a Muslim country, is supposed to be the "land of freedom"(*Achieved Utopia*), and it is heartening to see how Muslim woman is allowed to practise Islam without any trammels. As an American citizen, she has the right to vote and to voice her opinions. Rose Hamid, the woman mentioned, is one such American Muslim. This is not to say, however, that American Muslim women do not face prejudice, and Hamid is a good example of this. When she began covering her head recently, she was promptly fired by her company where she had been employed for last ten years. Such discrimination, even if unintentional, is rampant in the US.

In contrast, the Saudi women not only cover their heads, but also their faces and hands, and they are instructed to wear a black cloak known as the *Abaya* to cover their bodies. Saudi Arabia is perhaps one of the first Islamic nations in the world that implements the Islamic law to ensure peace and justice. Yet many of the laws in force, especially those geared at women, stem more from the patriarchal customs rather than being upheld directly by *Shariah*. For example, women are not allowed to sit in the front seat of a vehicle nor are they allowed to drive. Some non-Muslims may think of this as part of Islam while as it is more appropriate as a tradition or social norm. Nonetheless, that Saudi women are given certain privileges, which are quite unheard of in other Muslim countries, is highly remarkable. In accordance with Islamic law, Saudi women are offered dowries, often very high; and are entitled to keep their own wealth. Besides, they are almost never harassed because of protection provided by their families as well as government.

The fact remains that there is no country that really treats Muslim women the way they ought to be as stipulated in the holy Quran and in the light of Hadith. Painfully, the approach to women falls between the two extremes: one of complete hyper-orthodoxy, Taliban-type, and other absolute heterodoxy, Tukey-type. And this certainly is not what the Islamic way of living actually intends : the path of moderation. The holy Quran states—*Thus have we made of you an Ummah justly balanced, that ye might be witnesses over the nations (2: 143).*

From these words, it is amply clear that Islam aims at moderation in all spheres : beliefs, morals, worship, and all human affairs. In fact, its this moderation which, when carried over honestly in all aspects of life, constitutes *Siraat-ul-Mustaqeem* (the straight path).

All that is needed is to rejuvenate and reassert the status, which Islam has given to woman. This will have a positive effect on her psyche and will encourage her to participate more actively in the socio-economic affairs of the community. To achieve this goal, Muslim woman must be given adequate opportunities in the field of **Education**—both religious and secular—as required by *Shariah.*

That the best panacea that can come from nothing but the depths of holy Quran, from the teachings of holy Prophet (SAW) and the wealth of rich Islamic tradition, continues to elude the Muslims. Perhaps, this is one of the rankling tragedy of contemporary times in general and women in particular.

Moolah Not Morality

Dazzling. Defiant. Devious. These are catchwords for the contemporary Media. Creeping into the vitals of human existence, it is turning out to be all-pervasive. To the extent that all predictions about its puissance are falling short of its present prowess. Contrary to Mc Luhan's dictum that message is the medium, today the medium is the master. Even Alvin Toffler's *Future Shock* – the disease of change –could not be prevented. No matter how we try to pace our lives, the society as a whole seems to be trapped, unable to capture the unshaped media.

The 'invincible predominance' over public opinion and psyche often displayed by media has no parallels. From Gulf to Kargil or Afghan war, and Diana, Lewinsky affair or nearer home Arushi murder case– media has turned rapaciously calculated. That which even much touted *Soldier's Diary* or peeping-tom books like *Unlimited Access* by Gary Aldrich couldn't do. All this speaks of the possible media absurdity which is rapidly grabbing the world of opinions and ideas. However, in the process, media has ever profaned its very purpose. Not only it flunked out in its role as a catalyst for positive change, it has also resorted to means which are highly baneful for a healthy milieu in any society.

Some years back at Beijing, the fourth UN World Conference on Women adopted *A platform for Action* to force gender issues onto the global agenda. The success of the conference to a large extent was attributed to the world media. Unusually, the media for the first time exhibited an unprecedented thrust in its spot coverage, news and views alike. Analyzing the areas of dissent and controversy, and pointing around positive patches, media went all out to disseminate each and every deliberation at Beijing. Indian media, too, conducted itself creditably. It reported the proceedings and marked out the areas of future course of action vis-à-vis women issues, as outlined in the *Platform for Action*. Perhaps a sense of fatigue or tedium induced by the deluge of copy preceding and leading up to the Beijing event set in. Or else editors just felt that it was time to switch back to meatier and profitable pastures. Whatever the reasons, the media dried up considerably on issues relating to women and an immediate fall-out was that most major Indian national dailies withdrew their gender pages.

Contemporary newspapers present a grim and dismal picture when it comes to women's issues and news. The content is either negligible or compressed and truncated to just a few columns, mostly in the inside pages. More nauseating is the growing trend in media to portray women as victims. Some recent studies of news stories show that sex and sensation is the primary motivation behind the reportage. The study entitled *A Pressing Matter,* of four main English dailies in India finds that women's issues accounted for little over two percent of the total news items in one of the dailies and even less in the other three. The 'sensational' stories relating to women, which were invariably crime stories, got between 52 and 63 percent of news coverage.

The findings are more telling in a book *Women, Democracy and the Media*. Of the five major dailies included in the study, the books finds out that only 8 out of 584 editorials (1.4 percent) were on women's issues. This speaks volumes about the media's so-called prioritization. The brass tacks is that media can only 'exploit and enlarge' the real plight of women. It's not meant for alleviating the same.

Strangely enough it is media, the so-called protagonist of 'women's cause', which is brutally jettisoning the very survival of women in a society whose 'tastes' it panders and programs by commodifying none else but women! It is appalling that a reputed newspaper house like *The Time of India* (TOI) too resorts to such gimmicks to boost its sales, and perhaps its elitist image. The paper publishes a regular update on fashion and entertainment which has sneaky-coloured photographs depicting models and actresses in the barest minimum of clothing. And when they are 'dressed' it is more often than not in 'see-through' pieces. That such reading material is meant for the 'specific elite' may have many takers. But then what percentage of TOI readers would actually be seen in the kind of 'apparel' promoted and 'style' propagated. One fails to understand the logic behind publishing such regular stuff that passes-off in the guise of daily razzmatazz, as means for jacking up the circulation.

In a bid to be counted among the elite club, *The Asian Age,* also comes up with columns that serve as entertainment titbits about the lifestyle of the rich and the famous, the bold and the beautiful, and whose underlying theme is unquestionably 'erotica', even as it is cushioned by tags of food fads, home tips, agony aunts *et al.* The newspaper publishes denigrating and outrageous photographs even on the front-page. Its Olympics coverage was nothing short of soft-porno. No doubt, *The Asian Age* does present a wide range of news, views and analysis. Yet, to prove itself different and to break away from the traditional staid mould, it seems to have joined the ranks of those out to legitimize the commodification of women.

It's all too easy to dismiss such analysis yet another instance of 'middle-class mentality and morality'. Ironically, the media, particularly the print media, is dependent on this very middle class for its survival as it forms an important constituent of any developing nation. The media does owe a responsibility to the middle-class in order to ensure its own mental health. More so for any nation whose sense and sensibility has not yet reached the pits!

The debate that how media at large portrays women is all too clear and hackneyed that it's neither worthwhile nor fruitful to go on any further. Needless to mention, the world media lives by the maxim—"where commercial success is assured, spiritual bankruptcy is ensured." The only irony is that justification, theories, arguments and propaganda are put forth in defence of the indefensible.

The alluring yet fallacious premise that the 'taste' of people has changed over a period of time is just plausible. Who builds opinions of peoples the world over, who moulds the 'taste' of public and who conditions their thinking that they begin to take a thing, wrong in principle, as irrevocable set pattern that knows no boundaries and has no religion— it's all crystal clear.

Perhaps, the votaries of all this baseless argumentation would do good to take a closer look at the powers that control the media all over the world. Commerciality not philanthropy; moolah not morality is what governs the world of media, whatever the frequency of its being hot-gospeller and prurient!

Failed Goddesses

In Anton Chekhov's famous play *The Cherry Orchard,* Lopahin, a young merchant, describes his life of hard worked and success. Failing to convince Madam Ranevskaya to cut down the cherry orchard to save her estate, he goes on to buy it himself. He is the self-made man, who purchases the estate where his father and grandfather had been slaves. He seeks to replace the cherry orchard with summer cottages where coming generations will see a 'new life'. In elaborating his developmental vision, he reveals the image of a man that underlies and supports his activity–"At times when I can't go to sleep, I think: Lord thou gavest us unbounded fields and the widest horizons, and living in the midst of them we should indeed be giants." At this point, Madame Ranevskaya interrupts him, saying–"You feel the need for giants. They are good only in fairy tales. Anywhere else, they only frighten us."

It is said that perceptions regarding life and world depend in part on the relative position of the observer. The Chekhov's play suggests that when the observer is a woman, perspective may differ. All of us see things from diverse angles and this is true of women in particular. Sensitivity to the needs of others and the assumption of responsibility for taking care lead women to attend to voices other than their own and to include in their judgment other points of view. As such, women define themselves in a context of human relationship and judge themselves in terms of the ability to care. That's why, woman's place in man's life has been that of a nourisher, caretaker, helpmate, and a weaver of relations on which she herself relies. But what, when a woman makes a mishmash of her observations and roughly tangles the relations which she has weaved with her fragile hopes. Then indeed, she proves to be a bad observer as well as a failed manager.

So failed the so-called goddess of feminism Simone de Beauvoir. Some years back, the publication of her personal letters to one Nelson Algren, raised a storm. Apparently, the demystification of a significant kind had taken place. The image of this woman who authored the gospel of feminism, *The Second Sex,* was all but tarnished. She sought sexual, economic and political freedom for women across culture, so much so that an entire canon was created, inspired by her perpetual harangue to accommodate anyone who wished to talk about the fashionable "woman-question". However, revelations in her letters about the unconventional relationship with Jean Paul Sartre, eclipsed the 'halo' of the woman who fought vociferously for establishing the 'unassailable emancipation' of entire womankind. While ardent followers of her faith viewed the issue as a welcome humanization of their idol, her critics used it to malign her. The whole episode merited a closer look and a radical dissection. The moot point seemed the relevance or otherwise of an ideology whose creator faltered miserably. Above all, the brand of so-called feminism which she propounded, while being utterly helpless on personal front, brought to light the inherent fallacy of her ideals – that are unnatural and impracticable.

Needless to say, that an ideology which fails to be a salve to its originator, leaving its followers in wilderness, is too vivid a proof of its inefficacy. Beauvoir herself was the subject of a conflict that she sought to resolve through her cult, but ironically could not protect herself from– a problem that no flimsy theory in the world can address. She seemed to have had a parallel word of existence alongside her ideology: an existence that questions the ideology or worse still, the need to have it at all. It could be argued that Beauvoir's so-called feminism and her personal life were two separate worlds. The question that pops up is as to why Beauvoir didn't come out with this dilemma of hers during her life time. If nothing, such frankness would have certainly helped her followers resolve or at least be more comfortable with conflicts which they were and are afraid to reveal in public.

Strewn by her conflicting sense of moral duty as a woman towards two men– Nelson Algren and Jean Paul Sartre– Beauvoir failed to balance her mental being with her emotional existence. More so for a woman whose entire life was dedicated to the idea of 'emancipation'! Somewhere down the line, she must have felt guilty of playing ideological histrionics not only with herself but ostensibly with her camp followers all over the world. A decade after the death of Beauvoir, her phoney idealism looks askance for an obituary amongst the colossal junkyard of isms, cults and ideological hallucinations and aberrations.

It's said that those who speak loud, most of the times they speak hollow. And their hollowness is exposed only when their own selves get involved. The fate of so-called feminists is the same. Even as much do they waft in the breeze of 'liberalism' and long do they dance on the waves of 'emancipation,' they realize the inadequacies of a futile revolution that brutally dethrones women. Likewise, Shobha De, the *desi* brand of Beauvoir, has also learned her 'failed lesson'. Being mother of six children, she quickly realized that her advocacy of a permissive society might boomerang on her. She decided to pontificate in *Speed Post*, her autobiographical book: 'abstinence rather than protection'. She implored her daughters to learn to cook and shop, and 'solemnly entrusts the well-being of the girls in future to her eldest son'. Shobha prescribing male domination?!!! Sounds a bit lunatic. The 'sheet anchor' of Indian feminism turned the tables topsy-turvy. The feminists were gushing their teeth!

Nevertheless, there are feminists and there are feminists. The 'Lib of Tasleema Nasreen' is literally a lib in toto. Out to promote adultery and fornication, she looks upon home-keeping and child rearing as the worst forms of slavery. Women must therefore 'revolt' and act like the 'heroine' of her novel *Shodh* (Revenge). There is nothing latent or vague about the neo-hedonistic nature of her dirt-cheap feminine message. Her flagrant writings, inspired by nothing but her abnormal sexual behavior, have left no doubt about the fact that she behaves the way she writes, and she writes the way she behaves. During the past decades, she has divorced and married many men. But then, marriage and divorce have very little meaning for her, for she not only upholds promiscuity in the name of 'Women's Lib' but practices it in letter and spirit with no regrets.

Perhaps in her case, it's not yet a complete failure. The confession is still to come. May be it is not long before her own children will grow-up to inherit the kind of Bangladesh, whose moral and social fibre she relentlessly tried to slow-poison and pollute by her bullshit writings even when she stands expelled from the country. Surely, a god-damned situation for the 'goddess' like her or for that matter anybody of her ilk.

Down the ages, all man-made isms and ideologies have been found lacking mostly because of dichotomy of thought and action of their propounders. The posterity cast a questionable look on these 'man-made thought-systems' once they came to know about personal lives of their creators. Also, being man-made, the likely chances of any ideology being cent percent true and righteous was impossible for no human being can ever design and create a working model for mankind or a group within it. It is same like asking a marvellous machine to point out its inherent lacunae and strengths to draw up an operational model for itself. Such a working model in spite of its great mechanical precision can never be fool-proof. No doubt, this job can only be performed best by the creator or architect of this machine.

Therefore, the mantra of salvation lies in a God-centric model in all systems of universe and this immutable fact is taken care of only by a divine code based on prophetic revelation. Man–centric philosophies are nothing but symptomatic treatment that can at best provide transitory relief. Not salvation.

Between within & without

"No! I do not understand it.
But what is more important
to me is that
I understand Dr. Einstein".

One cannot but appreciate this prompt reply of Mrs. Albert Einstein as someone asked her if she understood her husband's theory of relativity. Actually, the woman behind the scientific genius like Einstein *was* what she was: creative in her own very valuable way. For her it wasn't imperative to decipher the dimensions of sci-logistics, as was the urge to read the mind of a man who was more a precious life-partner to her than a renowned scientist.

It happens that many a common people are often more sensitive and understanding than others. Possessing a low-profile, they may not be famous but they are incredibly creative. And this naturally simple fact has been substantiated even by various research studies. A. H. Maslow, Professor of Psychology and a researcher of note in the field of creativity, admits that when he first began to study the subject, he had unconsciously confined creativeness to painters, poets and certain scientists and inventors. Then Maslow met a woman who was uneducated, quite poor, and a full-time housewife and mother. She did not write fiction or dash off new scientific theories. Maslow says that yet she was a marvelous cook, mother, wife and homemaker. With little money, her home was somehow always beautiful. She was a perfect hostess. Her meals were banquets. In all these areas, she was original, novel, ingenious, unexpected, and inventive. And Maslow just *had* to call her creative.

As far as the grain of creativity is concerned, it is hard to believe that some decades back a knowledgeable critic would have cried out: 'We are in danger of developing a cult of the Common Man, which means a cult of mediocrity'. However, today we seem to be in a jeopardy of nurturing a cult of "Extraordinary Man, or for that matter, Woman" who have a tendency to overdo things in the rush of getting noticed or recognized. This has rendered the concept of creativity crackpot.

In relation to woman, her creativity is linked quite closely to her mind than any external agencies. The more her mind is trained, the more creative she turns out to be. Education, of course, is the best training. But the people who are concerned with the formation and stimulation of women's minds have a recurrent nightmare. They envisage one of their graduates suddenly confronting herself in a mirror at some point of her age.

In college, she had been a first class student. Teachers had praised her prose style, her insights into modern history, her keen grasp of economics and social problems. The question arises as to what she has done with her intellectual skills or, to say, her creativity. The grim answer is: nothing. She has either become a wife or a working woman. Why, she may be asking herself, did she go to college if this was the ultimate object or aim?

This may again smack of a dilemma as inner contradictions are not a new thing for women. On the home front, a woman had to be able to manage children and home. The attempt to play these roles, and at once remain 'feminine' produced its share of conflicts and anxieties. Nonetheless, it wasn't that painful. She had no part to play outside. Today, she is bifurcated between within and without. Consequently, her creative output suffers on both fronts. And this is happening despite the much talked about social, economic and technological changes now in process. The growing mechanization and automation of home can hardly help a woman to live an actively creative outside life. Too many promising professional careers on the part of women wither away at present before their high points have been reached. The woman, who enters a profession and then marries and has children, has to 'interrupt' her career which, in majority of cases, is rarely caught up later. She does not retire, but she resumes in 'piecemeal style'. This obviously tells upon consistent productivity and efficiency in her career.

The moot point, as such, is that if dual responsibilities will face her in the home and in her career (she is already facing them badly), what kind of education will prepare her to lead this 'double life' efficiently? What are the ways that will succour in the fuller exploration of her creative resources with ever-increasing fervour?

It is sad but unarguable fact that most human beings go through life partially aware of the full range of their abilities. In our society, we could do much more than we now do to encourage self-development. We could drop the increasingly silly absurdities dominating our education (this can be done by any educator/teacher on individual level), and devise arrangements for lifelong fruitful learning. Of course, we cannot question the credibility of anything that has been made to stay as infallible and unchallengeable. But if the 'dual-role' of women is now being accepted as something inevitable in our society, we have to chalk out and display alternatives for refuting its logic. And this can be easily done by those engaged in women's education. If the target group is itself addressed, it can be a result-oriented exercise. Educating women *properly* and then letting them decide for themselves their course of action, is far better than thrusting dictates on them. Compulsion works but only transiently.

Women's minds are one of the major resources for any nation. We should be determined to help them achieve the success they—and, of course, their community—need to make the pursuit of happiness and intellectual satisfaction a realistic goal. Creativity in them ought to be recognized and nurtured through healthy means.

Gender Gamut

They say women were invented just one short day after men. And now only recently, women have been discovered by social scientists. Thanks to their keen sight! Now apparently we are fair game, anytime, anywhere – dissected and discussed in the media under umpteen titles like *Modern Women in Transition, Whither the Modern Female, Women Outside, Women Studies, Women Logistics, Women Hours, Women Point* and *blah blah*. All this attention is surely gratifying. However, at times it's over-indulgent, making us suspicious about ourselves. Perhaps in the ensuing process, it also leads to unwanted controversies and conflicts, bordering on plumb nonsense, between the genders.

The oft-repeated, rather raged out, issue making the tongues wag *ad nauseam* is about 'career-oriented' woman. The duality of her role (as a wife and working woman) has become a favourite whipping horse for most of social scientists and experts, especially men. Honestly, there is no denying the fact that working women go in for various compromises and their identity as a whole is never complete. They are usually strewn between forces of natural and unnatural settings. There is hardly a balancing consensus in their living. They are always occupied, running and struggling to maintain peace with their private and public spheres. How far do they succeed, is a separate debate. Nonetheless, it too can be argued that how successful have men been at combining marriage with a career. Most men work and are married. Yet, how effective are they in this dual role? How efficient and happy? One can hardly say, because most men are completely unaware that it is a dual role. It never occurs to them that they might be expected to be anything but career men. It's taken for granted that the career man will neglect his children, ignore his wife and fall asleep after dinner. He tends to be selfish, perhaps unknowingly. He quickly forgets that a small feeling of putting oneself into someone else's shoes is what's most needed for an enduring mutual bond of love and respect, and of course, a strong family. A sincere realization, a kind word and a loving gesture is enough to alleviate all the onus of life together.

It is known that man would find it impossible to combine marriage with dish- washing or do baby-sitting. He wants his wife to manage everything smoothly from home-keeping to child rearing. A wife who is a good attendant to his children arranges for their schooling, irons their uniform, packs up their lunch, accompanies them to bus-stop; and waves a sweet goodbye only to return back home to serve him a hot breakfast; and see to it that his personal things, from socks to handkerchief, are kept in their proper place so that he can easily pick them up the moment he needs them, and then leave for his office in haste; least bothered about the poor soul who has yet to finish up the chores and then start going for her own job. A hell of a life! No rest, no respite. A mechanical survival.

Another premise generally discussed about women is their 'emotional instability'. Wavering in their stand and sentimental about their opinions: this jeeringly sums up women for majority of people. However, it sounds ludicrous. With utmost gravitas, the same can be said about men.

In fact, it can be a natural condition with anyone. As far as men are concerned, look at the record. Oedipus—would you say he was a well-adjusted boy? Hamlet—to be or not to be. Alexander the Great—a has-been at 30, unsatisfied. Napoleon, Karl Marx, Hitler. History teems with maladjusted men. Their 'escapades' and 'endeavours' have lifted the pages of history to a sardonic end.

Women can't be exonerated in this regard. History is replete with women whose greed, ambitions and perversities have no parallel. Ruthless rulers like Livia, Messalina or Cleopatra; scandalous wives like Catherine of Russia, Maria, Queen of Spain or Queen Tishyarakshita of Emperor Ashoka; fanatical admirer like Unity Mitford of Hitler; clever seductress Josephine of Napoleon; or latent lover Edwina of Nehru—women have left the indelible crappy stories behind.

All this smacks of the behavioural sloppiness of human beings – both men and women. All possess emotions as an indispensable part of survival. However, only the degree of 'control over emotions' varies.

As such, the relegating of 'emotional instability' only to women stands illogical and irrelevant. There is a whole gamut of internal as well as external systems coordinating the stability of emotions in any individual.

The finality of any debate or discussion related to women need not to be meticulously slanted. Rather, it would be better to refrain from such rigmarole, preventing complexity of very simple and minor issues. Besides, why can't men or women be happy just in being *what they are,* without drawing absurd comparisons? What more can anyone want out of life than to live it exactly as it has been gifted and ordained to us by Almighty? Or is it, just possibly, that simply *being* one's own definition is not a fit occupation for men and women of today's era? Maybe it's interesting to be either a man or a woman only when there is some basis for intelligent comparison. But then, each one of us with all finesse and faltering; pluses and minuses; whites and blacks; positives and negatives, constitute an entity worth reverence within respective spheres of influence and role-playing. No one among us should be abhorable, no one antagonistic. All people cannot be categorized among plug-uglies. Man and woman complement each other. There is no point of being argumentatively antithetical. Let's simply simplify our lives.

She shouldn't be born

Unaware of the fact that she was listening to everything they conversed, he continued to argue with his wife, "Trust me, I have heard of this doctor, he will solve our problem". Not willing to visit the doctor, she said humbly, "I am fine with whatever I have. More so, this is His wish and plan and I have full faith in Him. So I need not to have any consultation". The poor girl was surprised while listening to the argument between her parents. She could not comprehend the reluctance of her mother for not seeing the doctor. A sudden thrash…And a scream of her mother followed the shrill command of his father, "Are you coming to the doctor or else I kill you?" Frightened, the girl clutched herself between arms and closed her eyes. The poor girl was in absolute darkness, a void where she felt quite secure. Cuddled by her mother's pristine warmth, she was being nurtured the best by her. It was like procreating her on blood of admiration.

Sometime later, she heard a strange conversation and felt something moving over her as someone was mumbling, "Well, I am doing it but don't disclose it to anyone. Sonography shows that it is a baby girl." Two days later, she briefly saw the light of the brute world with shady people around. And then, she found herself dumped in the trash bin of one of the hospitals.

She did not find herself alone in the beautiful gardens of Paradise. Hundreds of ill-fated girl babies were there from times immemorial. "You are lucky enough to be killed so soon. You saw the brutality of your father and that is all." She turned towards the voice to see a young woman speaking to her, and before she could respond the young woman continued, "I died and lived thousands of times ever since my marriage at the hands of my in-laws", and taking a deep sigh she added, "and one fateful day, my husband burnt me alive." The gardens were full with women who were raped and then brutally murdered. It had scores of old women who breathed their last for the want of a glimpse of their missing son. She was not alone. She felt.

She was 'fortunate' to take a small sojourn to world and come back before the loathsome layers of world reality would dawn on her. She was not discriminated. Her childhood was not trounced. She was not mortified for growing up in an unsafe society. Nobody teased her. Nobody defaced her. Her marriage was not an overgenerous affair. Her parents were not squeezed to the hilt. Her in-laws did not abuse her and her life-partner could not kill her. So, she was spared of all this pain and punishment for being a 'fair sex'.

Why should this society bear girl child? For what? Breeding boys and nothing else?!! What a shame! Why lament aborting a female foetus? Why carp about sex determination tests and unabated horrific genocide? No reason can validate this madness. Rising crime against women defies the logic of women's survival.

Isn't it a high time we start thinking 'rationally' and stop emotional ranting? Kill a girl child before others pounce on and make her life hell. Sounds bizarre! But not as bizarre as molesting, raping and burning a woman.

What is the point of grooming a girl for a wretched end? The question may seem silly. And reckless too. But it is not. It simply underscores the reality of our society today. Our situation is not far from bleak and doomed to fail. The signs of this distressing reality are already being reflected. There is a general state of weakness and disarray. Society is supplying its 'standards' to the system. The standard of means and misuse; of morality and manipulation; of merit and mediocrity. As such, the crooked casing of our society markedly entails the collapse of the social system.

Unless society amends its way, the social system won't alter its course. Unless we collectively revive the virtuous acts of *amr* and *nahyy*—enjoining good and forbidding evil—the upsetting reality will haunt us. Ignoring the realities and mere bewailing won't do No society can achieve health without encouraging positive criticism of its leaders, institutions and individuals; and without sharply denouncing the bad practices. Unless we become a community of worth and cultivate a social ethic, to be a community that brings peace and security, and enables people to be a source of goodness and hope for all around them, is going to be a herculean task. It won't happen unless we move to the roots that bestow us our belief and identity.

India's Shame

The recent ruckus over the BBC Storyville documentary *India's Daughter* has thrown up an interesting debate. The subject of documentary is the December 16, 2012 fatal gang rape of a 23-year-old student and the movement that followed it. The documentary opens with uncanny reconstruction of the happening and then switches focus to the furious street protests that swept India in the wake of the incident. The documentary also features conversation with the parents of the victim and their accounts of her childhood. However, the interview with one of the accused, the driver of the bus where the attack took place, kicked up the row. As per CNN-IBN report, the accused, "awaiting a death sentence for his role in the attack, lays the blame for that night on the victim and makes derogatory comments about women and their place in Indian society. He does not flinch when filmmakers describe her gruesome injuries to him". The death row convict also claims in the documentary that his execution will endanger rape victims. The comments created a massive public uproar in India, with media pouncing on British filmmaker Leslee Udwin for defaming Indian society through *India's Daughter.*

Consequently, the documentary was banned by Indian court on the ground that excerpts "appear to encourage and incite violence against women". The goverment also asked Google to block its Youtube links from India.

The documentary was to be aired by BBC on the eve of International Women's Day (March 8) but was aired two day earlier, and was also premiered in New York at event in downtown Manhattan ahead of an airing on Public Broadcasting Service (PBS America) later this year. However, given the sharp reaction edging up from India, the BBC removed the documentary from Youtube and the BBC's online player does not now allow it to be watched outside UK.

Leslee Udwin, who has been accused of "violating law and not abiding by the agreement" with the Indian agencies which gave her necessary permission for the interview, retorted—"the Indian government should hang its head in shame for the ban. The banned documentary is a real reflection of what society thinks" *(India Today, 11 March-2015).*

Evoking shrill response from both Indian media and public, one of the Indian television news channels that had scheduled airing of the documentary was crudely castigated and accused of "angling for some international award" by rival channels.

Turning a blind eye towards graphic reality of rape in India, most of the media outlets in India as well as some highbrows, made an issue of 'national prestige' out of the BBC documentary. Jingoism was hammered to crack out the real issue of increasing violence against women by dubbing documentary as a part of "conspiracy by the west to tarnish India's reputation".

Of course, what the convict divulged before the camera seems quite absurd but it also points towards the general mindset in India regarding gender issues. How women are seen over the continuum of masculinity in India, especially in robust rural populace, remains an uncomfortable and unanswered question.

Many in the Indian media questioned the state of women in Britain, the place from where the documentary emanated, thereby shadowing the existing debate over the subject of the documentary. Amazingly, in response to *India's Daughter*, an Indian named Harvinder Singh claimed to have made a parallel film titled 'United Kingdom's Daughters', revealing that 250 women in UK are raped daily and the situation is much worse in other western countries. As per this documentary, one-third of Britons believe women are responsible for rape. It also claims that killing figures of victims are low in UK as women do not resist rape *(Daily Telegraph, 13 March-2015)*.

Statistics may be startling in other places as far as the crime against women is concerned but that does not seem to justify the happenings in any other country. The only difference can be in the way other societies look at rape victims. In America, such crime is alike to 'drinking a cup of coffee'. In other permissive societies, the crime is usually not reported at all. As such, debate varies as per the gamut of different existing societal norms. As such, for a country like India, drawing analogies may not help. It is to be about discrepancy between entertaining the westernization and breaking the façade of women empowerment, or else mapping out the real mindset of population.

Interestingly, coming to mindset, a concurrent contradiction demolishes down all the so-called distress shown by Indian media and intelligentsia towards *India's Daughter*. While the said documentary was being scoffed at, a video surfaced wherein a BJP member parliament Yogi Adityanath was promoting necrophilia in his public speech. He was appealing "Hindu men to dig the graves of Muslim women and defile their dead bodies by raping them" (indiatimes.com). No prime television news show was aired to slam such a communal and pervert mind. No analytical stories were done to denounce such a criminal call.

If a rapist bus driver's viewpoint raises hue and cry, what about a member parliament who propagates rape of dead women?! Isn't this India's Shame? When dangerous doublespeak invades the core of discourse in any society, then nobody can assure safety to anyone, not to speak of women alone. Criminal depravity and anarchy prevails. And nobody can ward off the doom of truly tarnishing nation's reputation. If only India's Daughter does not become the victim of India's Shame!

Generational Saga

A midget is a big world. High dreams, small hopes. Frivolous, yet sensitive. Strong but not bold. Weak but not fragile. Neither beautiful nor ugly. Brilliant not at all; moron never ever. Who's that? An average girl, or better say, a lady of my generation.

At every turn of life, she waits avidly for her entry into the new world: the world sans big profiles and bigger promises; the world sans the biggest plausibility.

In fact, *the new world* means many different things for her. It can be a wonderful experience, which touches deepest emotions. A quite understanding, mutual confidence, sharing and forgiving. A loyalty through good and bad times. The world that settles for less than perfection and makes allowances for human weaknesses. Harbours contentment with the present, hopefulness for the future and no brooding over the past. The day-in and day-out chronicle of problems, compromises, and disappointments amidst small achievements and little joys. Above all, the *new world* makes-up for the many things the lady has missed: maybe an innocent smile; a selfless gesture; the sincerity of purpose; and the significance of honesty in everything.

She's perhaps the lady who woke in bits, piecemeal over the years. She discovered herself and the world, and then forgot only to discover them again and again. The process of waking never slipped back, and never was she free of herself. Like flowing up and down from a trance, she lodged herself in an eerily familiar life already well under way. She was both observer and observable, an object of her own humming awareness. Was she evolving? May be. May be not. However, the challenges of life were never unwarranted. She wasn't killed as a child, she was allowed to survive. She wasn't discriminated, she was loved. Yet, life and love connoted an obscurely tough battle for her. Beyond the walls of her home, the rules involved in this battle were quite different. Life was tough; love was rough. It was all about cheap bargaining: of success, failure, virtues, vices, affection and apathy.

Education enlightened her. Experience enfeebled her. Books carried her away in to the spick and span world—the pure, chaste, unspotted and unadulterated. Every alphabet meant a sacrosanct ideal. Every word an inviolable law. But then, realities dragged her down to earth, and dust of expediency settled all over her. Hard faced ideals never breathed their last, but they somehow got blurred in void. Adeptly she could justify any damn thing!

She became independent. Emancipated. She is *Aaj Ki Nari!* An entity having loathsome eyes for failing ever to recognize what is actually what. Standing in the queues; running in the crowd; bouncing into the buses; jostling through the men –she's what she never dreamt to be. Chasing her world of desires, she wrongly lands somewhere else. A misfit in a mischievous world!

She's the lady for whom the fragrance of *henna* and fascination of bridal dress costs more than her means. The extinction of "Upright Species" leaves few choices for her to hitch on. And still, the price tag is the one she hardly can pay on her own. But even as the No-So-Right halfwits fancy being the best buy, the destiny somehow takes her to the place she is wrought for. She gets what she deserves;

good if good, bad for bad, and the Divine Law operates. The new world, now seeming tenable, proliferates out from the vagueness again. She truly understands the beauty and power of Providence. She respects the concept of legitimate and sacred oneness, and ventures out to play the multiple roles—that of a loyal wife, a dedicated mother, and most importantly, a conscientious human-being.

She treads different roads; encounters ups and downs; meets saints and sinners; laughs with the winners; weeps for the losers; lives for others; dies for herself; and ultimately fits herself into the portrait of a lady who's not an uncommon, unparalleled, unerring goddess but an ordinary soul designed for things even beyond her comprehension.

Assimilating much, asserting little, she learns, unlearns and relearns many a truth. Perhaps the secrets of life; reality of fangs; humbug of faces; joy of giving; sorrow of losing; pangs of death; panacea of birth; bloom of flowers; blight of leaves; pleasure of riches; plague of rags; and everything that comes in the way, she picks up gladly. From a cry-baby to a story telling granny, she remains a lady in obeisance: Loyal, Affectionate, Dedicated, Yearning.

The odyssey of life leads her on, on and on... The dimples vanish, the wrinkles visit. She remains unchanged. The mirth of childhood, halcyon of youth and autumn of old age—every phase adds to her queer versatility. Chivvying to be a typical weirdo, she keeps catching sunny hope in her palms, holding windy fortune in her breaths, and arresting invisible lustre in the cages of her smallish mind. She falters and slithers along the tortuous route of her life but eventually has a pleasant face-off with her own world.

Long last, she reaches where she has to. She lives only once and if she works it right somehow, that's fair enough for her.

The Lonely Dolls

In the beginning, said a Persian poet, Allah took a rose, a lily, a dove, a serpent, a little honey, a Dead Sea apple and a handful of clay. When he looked at the amalgam—it was a woman (William Sharp, in the *Portfolio*).

Surely woman is stuffed of different hues. There is everything in her, from obscure love to obdurate hate. Her mental and physical constitution is an issue *per se*. It interferes with the working of whole mankind. It manifests its logical and emotional presence beyond any doubt. That's why woman is seen in variegated shades, one in serene seraphic disposition and other a distraught despondent women.

Serenity and despondency are both discrepant. The base and summit of happiness is when a person is ready to be what one is. When one is not, then sadness naturally conquers him. Then one is obsessed madly and hopelessly with ephemeral spring rather than being interested in changing seasons– the thing that is not communed with the happier state of mind and the ever-changing scheme of realities. Then facts clash head-on with delusions and down comes the piffling little world of make-believe. The debacle disappears within certain time, but not before wreaking a mental disaster, which happens to be the torturous price of sheer credulity and lack of insight.

So goes the saga of *The Lonely Lady* a novel by Harold Robbins. The novel depicts the shortcomings of the highly developed society of America, the so-called melting pot of the world, which causes a woman to end her life in a state of unbearable solitude. It is the story of a beaut, young American woman baffled by the glitz and glam of the film world, abandons her married life to become an actress. Her femininity helps her to climb the ladder of 'success', swiftly touching the pinnacles of fame and wealth. Surrounded by every kind of creature comforts, she has a host of fans and admirers. But the climax of her 'success' does not bring her the inner peace, and inner joy, as she discovers the bitter truth that "fame has a way of fading, and friends a way of disappearing when they are needed most" (*The Lonely Lady*, p 448).

The novel is perhaps allusive to the plight of the Hollywood diva Marilyn Monroe. Writes Maulana Wahidudin Khan in his book '*Woman between Islam and Western Society*'- "Thanks to Monroe's extra ordinary attractiveness, she became renowned as the "sex goddess" of the Hollywood. Her films were all a tremendous success in that they never failed to draw enormous crowds. The last film she acted in was *The Misfits* —a title which, in a sense applied to her own life, because she frequently had a feeling of being out of place." Monroe actually had developed a sense of being inapposite in her flashy world, a feeling of being jammed in a dreary vacuum. In the midst of maddening crowd of her fans, she was virtually alone. Snapshots portraying her with a tooth paste smile were regularly published in the press. However, in reality, she was sunk in a mire of depression. Eventually, her psychological state reached a flashpoint and became agonizing. She committed suicide by taking an overdose of sleeping pills. Just 36, her slightly but debauched material world debunked, leaving her with no option to stifle the life forever: death overtook her dynamism.

No doubt death is tragic, but it's never meaningless. It reminds us of the facticity of existence. From death it is possible to learn some of the important lessons of life. Death is, therefore, a new beginning, a moment of learning. For example, with the death of Princess Diana, the nature of contemporary reality—its contradictions and pathologies, its promises and possibilities—all were experienced. Diana's death showed us the tragedy of being a celebrity in a media-centric world. Long before her physical death, the perpetual gaze of the culture-industry had already killed her. Her death exposed the West's obsession with sex and the hollowness of its civilization. It seemed to have lost its agenda. Its only pre-occupation, it appeared, was with mindless excitement and intoxication, as over-bearing paparazzi ruffled Diana to the last. Her flossy, scandalous personal life had become the so-called feast of reason for the footloose journos and dime novelists. First a woman and then a charming princess, her fate unravelled many a myth about the 'emancipated' prima donnas of West who are projected as the role-models for the rest of the world. Behind their glitter and gloss, there are stinking and sardonic images of these Barbie dolls who belong to everybody and, ironically, to whom nobody belongs.

Yes, such women have been released from bondage not only at home, but from any kind of obligation. A new promise, a new airy-fairy world, a new 'freedom' is assured. And this 'freedom' has also brought new tragic consequences. Loneliness is just one. It's painfully dawning on the protagonists of such 'freedom' that the ordeals of crassly competitive and immoral world are too overpowering for women to endure. Even the 'emancipated' Western women are realizing this harsh reality. Few years back, the famous American singer Celine Dion, who sang *My Heart Will Go On* for smash hit *Titanic,* announced her plans to take a long break after completing a concert tour in 2000. "I want to have a normal life", she confessed. Her hectic life with interviews-on-the-go and sold-out stadium concerts are decidedly not the rudiments of a "normal life". Dion being grateful for her success still longed for life's more pedestrian pleasures. She disclosed here penchant for cooking and shopping, apart from raising children.

It is, of course, a costly wisdom. The jaunty soprano Celine Dion has brought this wisdom by experience. And there is no doubt that the wisdom acquired as the result of experience could be acquired less painfully if we accept and ruminate over the good words and preferred knowledge of those who speak out of their experiences. But then, there are very few people in this world who accede to this without first tasting the bitterness of experience themselves. This is exactly what the Eve of East is doing. From Nazia Hassan, whose estranged life met an excruciating end, to Bollywood queenbee Madhuri Dixit who finally jilted all her prodigal fans only to marry an American settled doctor—the oriental woman tastes what occidental woman has already vomited back! It seems that the Eve of East has come to understand that it is better to learn from others only after suffering.

How paradoxical, how foolish!

A Creative Symphony

'Middle Age' is the poem which introduced her to me. My 12th class English textbook carried it and I remember how curiously I liked the poem only to narrate it often to my mother whom I always found ironing clothes and preparing food for me and my brothers *ala* the poetess. A sense of intimacy really pervaded through her lines. Kamal writes, "Middle Age is when your children are no longer friends but critics, stern of face and severe with their tongue. It's the time when like pupae they burst their cocoons and emerge in harsh adult glory, and they no longer need you except for serving tea and for pressing clothes. But you need them all the same, and badly too, so that when left alone, you touch their books and things, and weep a little secretly".

Kamala Das belonged to Kerala, God's own Country. She had a penchant for poetry since early age, primarily because of the influence of her uncle and mother, both of whom used to write. Having no formal education, she was educated privately till the age of 15, when she got married. It is reported that because of the huge age difference between Kamala and her husband, he often encouraged her to associate with people of her own age. Thats why when she wished to begin writing, her husband supported her decision. And as she cruised along the path of creativity, touching new heights, she always found her husband as a great support. She once stated that "there shall not be another person so proud of me and my achievements". After he passed away, feeling insecure and missing a principled man like him, she wrote in *A Widow's Lament:* that he was her sunshade and home.

Kamala Das published many novels and short stories in English as well as in Malayalam under the pseudonym of *Madhavikutty*. Some of her work in English includes the novel *Alphabet of Lust,* in addition to five books of poetry, the one *Only* the *Soul Knows How to Sing* co-authored by Pritish Nandy.

In a paper titled 'Kamala Das: Creating a Voice by Seizing and Reinterpreting Religious Tradition' by Shoshana M. Landow (Anthropology 302, Princeton University, 1989), she writes that "Kamala's autobiography *My Story* tells of intensely personal experience including her growth into womanhood, her quest for love and her living in matriarchal rural South India after inheriting her ancestral home. Kamala has created a paradigm for the away repressive societies fear women's speaking, writing and other self-defining forms of personal expression. Like European women authors, Kamala seizes control of the society's own cultural codes, particularly those formed by dominant religious ideologies. She uses, for example, the terrifying religious images of *Kali*, the goddess of war and destruction, in her defiant reaction:

"I hung a picture of *Kali* on the wall of my balcony and adorned it daily with long strings of red flowers, resembling the intestines of a disembowelled human being. Anyone walking along the edge of my paddy field a furlong away, could see the Goddess and the macabre splash of red. This gave the villagers a fright" *(My Story,* p-201)."

Kamala often thus uses traditional religious imagery to sustain herself, besides passing a subtle satirical reference to whatever she observes. She always reaches into her own inherent religious tradition to find support for her defiant individuality. In her verses, the uncanny honesty extends to her exploration of womanhood and love.

In a book 'Kamala Das: a critical spectrum' by Pier Paolo Piciucco, it is maintained that her views can simply be characterized as a gut response, a reaction that, like her symphonic poetry and salubrious columns, is unfettered by other's notions of right and wrong. Transcending the role of a poet or a writer and simply embracing the role of a very honest woman, Kamala Das only celebrated the joyous potential of her genius while acknowledging its concurrent dangers without any hanky panky: "If you were to ask me which of my characters is the strongest, I would say myself. I certainly believe that a creator leaves a part of himself or herself in the creation. You can't escape that. You remain there trapped within your creation and that is the most vital part in creation. So certainly in my poetry, in my stories, a part of myself is there".

Kamala's achievements extend well beyond all this also. She had filled her life with as many experiences as she can manage to garner. Her intellectual acumen has been recognized so well that her poems are taught throughout India and even in foreign universities. She was a visiting faculty member abroad. Her columns gave her tremendous recognition.

She also took a dramatic decision to convert to Islam and adopted the name *Surayya*, which means the star Pleiades. The old lonely widow whose children had left her, had disclosed that for long she had no religion and remained an unclaimed parcel with the address stamped on it. 'There should be someone to claim me'—she had declared. And again as an undaunted creative genius whose voice has been redolent of nothing but honestly, she converted to Islam without bothering about any kind of subsequent ostracism.

Of course, creative people know well the game of life, but above all, they know best how to play it with an honest bravery. Mind it, bravery not bravado! Influenced by their own observations and experiences, they draw their own conclusions and judgments. Kamala Das nee Kamala Surayya had done just the same when she announced–*'Allah is good enough for me'*.

We: the Change Agent

Edmund Burke said-'All that is necessary for the forces of evil to win in the world is for enough good men to do nothing.'

But evil also triumphs when good women also do nothing. In her book 'Letters to a Young Feminist' by Phyllis Chesler, professor of psychology and editor-at-large of 'On the Issues' magazine writes, "You must become radically-compassionate toward yourself. This is hard, not easy, to do. Both men and women owe women large measures of radical compassion. Women often withhold this resource from each other, or dole it out as if it were a scarce commodity. And then, only to those women who do not threaten us". But this has to be forsaken, keeping in view the plethora of problems women are enmeshed in. The present-day women's challenge is in a new realm, that of the mind and spirit. She must find ways to better realize her worth, her intellectual contribution to herself and to society at large. This exacting endeavour cannot be achieved in isolation or in a confused state of mind.

Women need to come together, form small groups, and interact fruitfully with each other. Communication is paramount. Exchange of ideas matters. It opens new ruminative vistas for us while clearing suppressed doubts, fears and confusions we harbour unwittingly. These small groups maybe based on a specific need(e.g., working women's issues, career problems, family break-up, divorced females, bereaved mothers, widows, orphans, etc)or on a generic need to simply come together. Listening is vital, and it's possible when we come closer.

Author Nellie Morton writes about "listening a woman to her story"—listening with compassion so intently that her story naturally flows from the speaker, who feels heard and honoured. In her article 'Circles: Arms of Support' Ellie Lindsay mentions about the feeling of belonging that settles in... "We can safely express ourselves and simultaneously learn from others as they open to us. We come to know ourselves and each other, learn how to love and accept love, and believe that we can face a crisis because we have loving support. We can expose our wounds, cry until we are finished, and, in the nurturing context of the group, allow the healing process to begin. The group can become a laboratory for trying new ideas and ways of interacting—a microcosm of our world. A place where we are safe to experiment. We learn that even though we may be having diverse experiences, we are not different for we all have pretty much the same feelings. We all are not bereft of anxiety and problems. We stop feeling alone; we stop hiding. And we feel a sense of relief".

However, it's wise to remember that any support, group is not a miraculous therapy group. We are not propagating 'groupism'. We don't have to launch umpteen groups, name them, fund them, and set going in for 'publicity letter heads'. Support groups should be local, unnamed, unstructured. They should evolve naturally within our immediate ambience and limit itself there only. We don't even have to call them 'groups'. It should be an emphasizing exercise: meeting silent minds, making them open up, express their predicament, and then lending them succour in some small ways. It's simply sharing of things, especially in a society that has underwent a cataclysmic trauma because of a historical conflict. In the words of Lindsay, "It's a knowing, a connection with ancient roots, a deep self-assurance, a firm belief in ourselves and our causes, all of which draws us, eventually, to take our experiences and knowing to the outside world. With strength gained from the collective, our visions expand, doors open, and we dare to do and be such as we did not dream we could".

Every day we are confronted with shock stories. The unnatural and unpredictable things are happening with us. Everything is running beyond speculation. We need to pull together from this rubble a new society, a new world. We can discover some panacea in a world gone out of control or simply gone nuts. For that we have to first listen, and then float our cherished ideology in a way that it proves ambrosial. Herein lies our test, our challenge. To quote again Phyllis Chesler, "Towards this task, you have to move beyond words. You must act. Do not hesitate because your actions may not be perfect, or beyond criticism. "Action" is how you put your principles into practice. Not just publicly or towards those more powerful than you, but also privately towards those less fortunate than you. Not just towards those who are far away, but those with whom you live. If you're on the right track, you can expect some pretty savage criticism. Trust it. Revel in it. It is the truest measure of your success".

So, don't hesitate to create your woman space. Stand by what you mean. Don't dither. The world needs you as you need it.

Let her live

Consoler she definitely needs. And that too, from her own gender: the one who was brutally snatched from her before she could take her into lap and squander all her caress. She couldn't help; she had to be a mute spectator. She simply switched off, emotions relapsed, hope resigning to the inevitable. The little angel, a baby girl disappeared into oblivion. No one asked where she is, what has happened to her. No one heard her birth blubbery, not even her swan-song. For others she was never born and hence, she never died. But for someone writhing in maternal pain, she was much more than any unborn reality done to an unbelievable death. She was a pristine wish, a delicate dream, a nascent flower nipped in the bud.

For decades, millions of girls have been victims of so-called female infanticide, mostly in South and East Asia. In some third world countries, the sex ratio is dramatically lower. In India, there are 914 women to every 1000 men (Census, 2011).

India today tops the list in illegal abortions and female infanticide in the world. A UNICEF report says 50–60 millions girls have gone 'missing' in India in 1990. They are termed as missing as they were either murdered at the time of their birth or within few hours of birth.

In an article titled 'Women's Right in Islam: Modernising or Outdated?' Dr. Zakir Naik quotes-"In a BBC documentary film titled *Let her die* shown in the programme "Assignments", the statistics of female infanticide was given by Emetic Buchanan. It has to be a Britisher who came all the way from Britain to give us the statistics and make a documentary film in a country which has the maximum rate of female infanticide in the world. According to the statistics compiled by them, everyday more than 3,000 foetuses are being aborted in India on being identified that they are female. If you multiply this figure with the number of days in a year (365 days) we understand that more than one million female foetuses are aborted every year in India. It is practised maximum in the state of Tamil Nadu and Rajasthan. There are big bill boards and advertisements saying "Invest Rs.500/- and save Rs.500,000, signifying that you do tests like Amino sentesis or ultra sonography which cost about Rs.500/- and on identifying the gender of the foetus if it is a girl you can always abort her and thus save Rs.5,00,000/- which is usually spent in the upbringing of a girl and giving dowry in her marriage".

It smacks of typical *Baniya* mentality! Forget Beauty Pageants and Women's Reservations, –the reality is piquantly different in simon-pure India. Genetic testing for the purpose of sex determination and sex selective abortion, though officially outlawed, has become a booming business in India. It has grown into an Rs.1000-crore country wide industry. In May 2000, Indian doctors brought to the attention of the International Community the abortions of two million female babies per year.

A well researched book *Genocide of Women in Hinduism* by Sita Agarwal blatantly exposes "the single most anti-woman civilization in the history of world, whose followers she labels as mindless male supremacist pigs who know nothing better than how to burn their own wives and rape their own daughters". She cites the examples of Rajputs and Brahmins in Rajasthan and Tamil Nadu respectively, where practice of female infanticide has been rampant. Her treatise, in fact, is a vitriolic attack on one of the ancient religions of world, whom she unhesitatingly snubs as "truly inhuman".

As per Sita Agarwal, the history of female infanticide in India can actually be traced back to the Vedic period. The Vedas prescribe an intense hatred against women, and female children were considered highly undesirable in the nomadic Aryan patriarchal view. There is explicit sanction of female infanticide in Vedic religion:

"Hence reject a female child when born, and taken up a male" (Taittirya Samhita VI.5.10.3).

The instances of gender discrimination area also found in the writings of Manu. The guiding philosophy is that the female is under the custody of males from womb to tomb. Fully one-tenth of each generation of females is exterminated due to Hindu Laws *(Female Infanticide in India, Report By Manushri Bahukhandi)*. That during the first 50 years of independence more than 50 million girls have been killed in India, confirms the estimate of 1 million girls being murdered each year. By comparison, all other genocides in world history pale into insignificance. The Nazi genocide of Jews was only 5 million; the mass murder of 50 million female children has thus been *ten times* more severe than the Jewish Holocaust!! And the despicable killings continue.

But then, the enigmatic question arises about those who also indulge in this scandalous crime while claiming to be the followers of a faith which ordains high value and regard for a girl child. Hypocrisy is more discreditable. The interim census report (2011) indicates that J&K, a Muslim-majority state, has witnessed the dramatic and largest decline in sex ratio for the past one decade. The provisional data shows that the child sex ratio has fallen from 941 in 2001 to 859 in 2011. It is surely a grim and shameful scenario. The BBC news report says, "The Kashmir Valley, which has been in the grip of an armed insurgency against Indian rule for the past two decades, has now turned on its girls, killing them ruthlessly, in most cases even before they are born"*(Kashmir Killing Fields, 23 May-2011).*

That abhorred past is insidiously returning through a new door with new poses and new players, is a fitting parable for unabated female infanticide in this worst part of the world. "It is shocking to note that our society has graduated from a girl child-friendly to a girl child-hostile society... The mushroom growth of unregistered clinics and nursing homes within the state bears testimony to the fact that a sizeable number of medicos and para medics are indulging in malpractices. There are many abortion clinics, as these could be best described, running clandestinely which have grown in numbers during last two decades"*(Editorial Greater Kashmir, 25 April- 2011).*

So, modern science has just facilitated the ghastly exercise. From the ages when a girl child was burned alive to the times when she is not even allowed to see the light of the world—things have changed only for worse. Arrogance and hidebound attitudes are yet tackier elements of human civilization. All the goody-goody talk of human rise, evolution, progress, development *blah blah,* seem nothing more than a pure twaddle, more of a delusion perhaps.

Time demands that if we deem ourselves 'human', let's then behave as such. Let's sincerely harbour a belief that whoever brings up a girl child properly and kindly shall surely enter paradise *(Sahih Hadith, No.392).* Let a girl child be allowed to live: live to discern the changing colours;

the sky-blue pink and night-sable black; tints of pleasure; shadows of pain; fury of umpteen tornadoes; reverie of ephemeral stillness; façade of ups; fate of downs; taste of tears; pungency of smiles and much more.

Let her live, face the world, meet the vicissitudes, and slug it out stoically.

Characters Cry

Cinderella is simpleton. An unlucky girl with disregarded merit and beauty. She is despised because she is not cunning. She is maltreated because she is not pretentious. Her step-sisters give her hell and even get their eyes pecked out by doves out of malice. But Cinderella endures everything silently until fairies come to her succour and magic turns wind in her favour. More precisely, it's a magical windfall and the fairy tale ends. Cinderella lives happily ever after.

Even today fairy tales end on happy notes. One of the most successful contemporary revisions is Frances Minter's light-hearted *Sleepless Beauty*. Written in verse and exquisitely illustrated, it stars a resourceful Beauty who saves herself and also gets her prince.

This Beauty grows up in a swank Manhattan apartment. After she pricks her finger on the needle attached to an old time vinyl record player brought by a witch who crashes her 14th birthday party, she falls asleep. However, in this tale, Beauty calls the shots.

Beauty writes a thank-you note to the comely rocker whose music helped her fool the wicked stranger. They meet, and the rest is a fairy-tale history.

Sleepless Beauty has an interesting crunch in it: the witch is creepy, the threat is real, and Beauty triumphs romantically in the end. The whole tale reworks just one popular rendering of *Sleepless Beauty* – a sage of many incarnations. Unlike a passive heroine Cinderella, there is a progressive twist in the character of Beauty who is a 'doer', subverting traditional scenarios in order to skewer the values that Cinderella reinforced sometimes back.

This paradigm shift, even in fairy tales, implies many a point. The foremost is that the world is not same. And it won't be ever. Change is something inevitable. Cinderella has not died. The fact is that she is no more wanted. An embodiment of virtues, a paragon of truthfulness, and a byword of nobility—Cinderella is confined to archives. Beauty has stolen the march. She is on the stage, glittering under the flash-bulbs, swaying the world with her bold persona. Yes, she's bold!! Rather *bold and beautiful.* No hang-ups, no hesitations; striking the iron when it's hottest, unmindful about burning of fingers and carrying the day impudently. This is the quintessence of Beauty. Witches won't stop her and world she won't leave. Pain she cannot endure but prince she can entice.

The character of Beauty is all-alluring. Don't think she is 'Revamped Cinderella'. She is Beauty out and out. No white dress, no long hair, no golden wings, no magic wand: Beauty is bereft of all such frippery. She is more or less a playboy. She thinks not of bees and butterflies, but burgers and burgundy. She dreams not of flowers and fragrances, but of fads and fans. Reason is her anathema; ardour her manna. Love is her pet dog; lust her pet toy. She is the fast worker for she knows the art of fast-talk. Relations matter only when they suffice her interest. She is faintly amused to see emotions fluttering aimlessly in the dust. Time is her slave, she rides it like a queen and whips it like a sturdy horse woman.

Cinderella is antipathic. She is everything save Beauty. Her image evokes no razzle-dazzle. She has gathered an anachronistic halo. She is no oil painting but she symbolizes something living, pulsating and seeing. Small wonder, Cinderella today seems unhappy even as her tale has been rolled up, long back. She is witness to the pitiful devaluation of her character. Every aspect belonging to her has met a steep downslide. Something really seems jinxing Cinderella. Her spoiled rival Beauty has rendered her a cockshy. People disdain her. She fails to appeal their ogling eyes and appease their sentimental loitering. More pathetic is the way she feels sorry about her generation that has morphed into sheer "also-ran generation."

Perhaps, Cinderella epitomizes something that is never ancient history. Some characters remain as ever. They don't just represent any airy-fairy thinking but there is a complete ideology behind them. Mr. Man Friday of Robinson Crusoe is still a password of loyalty. Dr. Jekyll and Mr. Hyde still depict the duality inhuman nature. Lucy of Wordsworth still resonates selfless love. Characters are not mere contrived creations, they are connatural conceptions. They are born because they exist somewhere around, and keep existing endlessly with several changing add-ons.

So, no pink elephants around. Cinderella sans a fairy touch is a jolly decent girl existing in our tangible, real world in a miniscule proportion. She is anguished and concerned about us: the one of her ilk. The truth is that we aren't like Cinderella. We've changed our roles and we've come a long way since *Sleepless Beauty*. Even though we hold on to smiles and songs, dreams and desires, we actually make lots of hard choices and cry fewer tears. Stolidly oriented, we see nothing beyond mirrors. We don't deserve Cinderella's concern. She needs not to feel pity for us. She should value and preserve her tears for some good cause.

Please Cinderella, don't cry for us!

Beyond barbarity

According to Jewish folklore, Adam had two wives. The first was Lilith. She was banished from the Garden of Eden when she refused to make herself subservient to Adam. When she was cast out, she was made into a demon figure, and Adam was given a second wife Eve, who was fashioned from his rib to ensure her obedience to him.

There are also other folktales describing how Lilith captured Jewish babies in night and ate them, and how she led young girls and boys astray. Although Lilith was demonized by early Jewish culture as a symbol of promiscuity and disobedience, many modern Jewish feminists see Lilith as a positive figure: a model of woman as equal to man in the creation story.

In general parlance, Lilith is a hag who gives jitters to every noble soul, and firmly establishes her notoriety. She exists as a votary of evil, responsible for every misfortune that strikes the mankind. Her being a woman is the only fiducial point that connotes a subtle meaning.

The fact is that there is no let up in stories and doctrines which profess such absurdities regarding woman. It's at times disgusting to see how the image of woman is hackled and humiliated by illogical concoctions.

If someone breaks his bones, why blame a woman? If you bang your senses out, why incriminate fair sex? Why chide her for the sins you dabble in with open eyes and arms?

Why snub her for the blunders you commit so bravely? Why flog her for something where man is an equal sinner by being a self-appointed barbaric ruler?

Woman was never meant to be an object of 'enticement'. She never compels a man to fall for her, and fall so cheaply. She never demands a maniacal devotion from him. In fact, the forces that drive any man nuts are very nearly as irrational and unjust as those by which it makes any woman blindly and arrogantly possessive about something. The fault lies in the assumption that men, congenitally deemed rational, is drawn into a dragnet by a woman who is generally bereft of stable and sound mind. This style of drawing distinctions between male and female nature is not only largely arbitrary and often pure superstitious hogwash, it is absurdly beside the point. We perhaps ignore the essence of *human* nature. The imperative question is not whether women are or are not less logical by nature than men, but whether education, effort and the abolition of our illogical assuming and presuming can improve on nature and make them (and, incidentally men as well) more logical. What distinguishes human from any other animal nature is its ability to be unnatural. Logic and rationality are not natural or instinctive activities; but our nature includes a propensity to acquire them.

Woman is certainly not from an infallible species. At times, she too lives meanly like ants, and fights with cranes like pygmies. Even today it rankles as to why Jane Austen didn't marry her savior Mr. Darcy; why Emily Bronte died so young; why Emily Dickinson flitted; and why Christina Rossetti looked at life through the wormholes in a shroud.

There is a numbing paradox lurking in woman's nature: the same questions, the same answers, the same dilemmas, the same defiance, the same fears, the same hopes, the same delusions, the same realities. The worst is the sameness of suffering of stigmatization in the face of ridiculous allegories, analogies, doctrines, theories, and of course, shaggy-dog stories *ala* Lilith's attached to her.

Women cannot be branded as some separate special species or some subclass of humans. She is as angelic as any man could aspire to be by ennobling his conduct, and at the same time can be as beastly as any male by falling to abysmal depths of *Asfal-a-Safileen.*

Woman is neither a *'holy cow'* to be revered nor a *dassi* of her earthly *Parmeshwar,* nay she any longer needs to be declared as endangered species. She is not to be for granted as a cabbage-head factotum. She has to deliver at all fronts in the dynamically changing world and come up to mark in all aspects – not by condescension, reservations, quotas, rhetoric of MCP's and malafide glorifications of voyeuristic literati. She has much more at stake than to cry and wail over her stature on some nondescript date fixed by her Western mentors.

Woman has to live life every moment beyond the ludicrous myths and unjust decrees that try to advocate an ideology which is proving to be nothing but all gas and gaiters. Life, with all its searing pain and soothing pleasure, calls to her every moment. There is no time and scope for her to squander on trivialities and weepy stories – be those foolishly sentimental or hide-boundly temporal. This is something on which there should be no futile arguing because woman cannot afford it.

Crime against women

We really live in absurd times. Our reason seems to have gone gaga alongwith the forbearance to digest truth gracefully. Mere symbolism has become our rescue slogan. It gets all the more ludicrous when people attach moral sensibility to sheer growing of long beards or covering of heads. Had this been the criterion, the ethical dilemma in some of the Muslim countries where beards and headscarfs are quite universal, won't be the sizzling issue.

A matrimonial ad about a few Saudi and Kuwaiti men with HIV positive, was published few years ago in one *Sayidaty* magazine, a sister publication of *Arab News*. In response, a young woman sent a letter to the magazine, offering herself for the marriage. The magazine staff was surprised and conjectured that the lady might be mentally ill or was casual about the offer. However, to get the real thing, the magazine traced her whereabouts and interviewed her on the condition of anonymity. It was found that she is quite young veiled woman from Riyadh. She was a divorcee and had six children. Her fateful odyssey started at the age of 16 when, after finishing her prep school, she was married to an old man.

It was a marriage of convenience since her family lived in abject poverty. The old man practically jailed her and also warned her against socializing. After some time, she came to know that her husband was already having two wives and 16 children. Nonetheless, she carried on, and in the span of seven years gave birth to six children. The things took an ugly turn when old sheikh decided to marry-off her eldest daughter, just nine years old, to a 44 years old man to get rid of some of his debts. She gave in on the condition that he would divorce her immediately after her daughter's marriage. The old man agreed and divorced her.

The story developed further when this woman remarried secretly a rich man, aged 51, looking for a better life for herself and her children. After eight months of marriage, her second husband also divorced her for sake of keeping his first wife and children. Alone, she struggled to feed her children and seeing no alternative, she was willing to marry even a HIV patient – which was nothing short of suicide. She was virtually embracing death so that she may live.

The said magazine communicated her wish to meet one of the HIV patients. He welcomed the offer initially but later on backed out on being informed that she was married twice and had six children.

This is not a poignant tale of only one woman, but hundreds of her ilk who are victims of worst kind of oppression in countries wherefrom otherwise the best treatment towards women should get reflected in all aspects. Inexplicable atrocities are inflicted upon women, and worst still, justified and defended in the name of religion.

The fact is that such incidents can never be sanctioned by religion. That ignorance piled up with arrogance has made people misinterpret and misrepresent religion, is another tragedy. Women continue to get charred in the cauldron of dogmas and dictums that have no religious backing whatsoever. The ugly fact remains that not all is well with women in countries which should have been role models in this respect. And given the glorious period of

Islamic Governance they witnessed and flourished in, it becomes all the more paramount. Conversely, in the present situation, it's a tall order to expect Muslims to act as saviours when their own house is not in order. Political expediency, parochialism, shift of emphasis, and trivial issues being projected as major priorities, are some of the vital causes of decline and disintegration of Muslims as a community. As such all that is guaranteed to women by Islam and the Holy scriptures in a practicing, if not ideal, Muslim society seems to be an elusive dream.

Needless to point out that plight of women is no better in non-Muslim nations, and studies in this regard are more shocking and shameful. That practices like *Sati, Lausa, Devidasi, Niyog, Asura*, etc., continue to flourish in some parts of Indian is an open secret. That hapless, poor and socially deprived women of Bangkok, Burma and Nepal constitute a major chunk of that 'workforce' called sex-workers is not a hidden fact.

As far the Europe and America, the less said the better. The dream of 'emancipation' continues to take a heavy toll and tyranny against women is registering new highs, spreading in newer hues and breaking all the past records.

The current moral mess in Kashmir is a part of same story, except the inclusion of conflict element which has aggravated the scenario, making it more grim, dismal and disguising. The people who are addressed by Holy Quran as: *'Ye are the best of Peoples, evolved for mankind, enjoining what is right, forbidding what is wrong'* (3:110), seem themselves to be in dire straits, let alone their guiding other peoples. When even the very small dealings of their daily lives cannot be in sync with any set of moral guideline, the talk of reform at any level seems silly.

What we can do is to hang our heads down in shame, without justifying our duplicity and deceitfulness under the garb of symbolism or chop logic. Let's accept that religion has not touched us, not to speak of loving and living it. Mere Friday sermons, construction of numerous mosques, visiting shrines, growing of beards, covering of heads, floating *Maslaki Jung* (Sectarian battle) for self-supremacy—are no indispensable indicators of righteousness. The prevailing moral catastrophe around us is a testimony to it.

She's Mouj

How sweet, tender, pleasant and perfect is this word *MOUJ* (mother). It brings all aromas with itself. The love in its pristine form; the affection at its zenith. The power which runs with the tempest; rises with the volcano; smiles through the lips of the roses; and sings with the brooks. A pulsating heart akin to primeval dale that echoes all voices, the thumping soul that kindles all hopes : A mother, she is. As they rightly say "Who ran to help me when I fell. And would some pretty story tell, or kiss the place to make it well? My Mother!"

That mother is a woman, is an attribute *per se.* And to be a woman, as such, is a blessing. In fact, mother is an embodiment of all womanliness. She is loving because love is ingrained in woman's nature. She is sober because sobriety is aligned with woman. So, a mother is what a woman is: the kind perhaps depicted best in words by Khalil Gibran in his *Thoughts and Meditations.* It is the story about a friend of his, a youth desperate and lost on the path of life. One day, Gibran receives a letter from him, asking for a rendezvous. On meeting him, Gibran is surprised to see his friend having changed drastically. Enquiring about it, his friend replied – "Ay, my friend, the spirit descended upon me and blessed me. A great love has made my heart a pure altar. It is woman, my friend—woman that I thought yesterday a toy in the hands of man—who has delivered me from the darkness of hell and opened before me the gates of Paradise where I have entered. A *true woman* has taken me into the Jordan River of her love and baptized me. The woman whose sister I disrespected through my ignorance has exalted me to the throne of glory. The woman whose companion I have defiled with my wickedness has purified my heart with her affections. The woman whose kind I have enslaved with my father's gold has freed me with her beauty. The woman, who had Adam driven from Paradise by the strength of her will, has restored me to Paradise by her tenderness and my obedience."

Needless to say, the Biblical notion that Eve was first deceived and she was, thus, responsible for the Fall of Adam, is absolutely preposterous. The Adam and Eve were deceived simultaneously and were equally responsible for the deed. In Christianity, Eve is the first mother who brought eternal Hell, but in Islam it's she who has opened the door of Paradise, as it lies at her feet. She's a *Muhsanah*—a fortress against Satan and better than 1000 men. There is an innate sense of motherhood in her for she wants all her good virtues and qualities to be practically visible and preserved in generations to come. As enunciated by Napoleon—'The Future destiny is always the work of the mother.' Her lap is the first school, and her words the first prophecy. Her heart is the finest home and her mind the happiest playground. With every heart beat of child, her heart beats alongside. For every pulse, her pulse races faster. She is excited when her child crawls, and overwhelmed when it speaks in architecture of those broken syllables. Absolute completeness, absolute compatibility: it's the world of oneness, existing only between the mother and the child.

However, this sense of oneness, like many other intangible human-feelings, is fast losing out its meaning and necessity. Today, families are rampantly being nuclearized. Often, both parents work full-time and their children are, in effect, raised in crèches, kindergartens and nursery schools where hired baby-sitters and teachers take the place of mothers. It is obvious that these 'mother-substitutes' fail to meet all of the children's psychological and emotional needs. Consequently, not only do children suffer but the whole edifice of nation is rendered weak and flawed.

Besides, man and woman are both biologically and psychologically different. They are not equipotential in life. But when the woman is loaded with economic and social responsibilities along with the man, she inevitably throws off the burden of her natural duties. She fails to play the role which Nature has assigned to her. She, in vain, tries to equate herself with man and endeavours to express manly instincts in her conduct. Thereby, bringing her own life as well as humanity to grief. The same catastrophe is narrated accurately in *No Thanks, Baby,* the write-up by some Western lady Eleanor Mills which appeared in *The Spectator* some time back. Eleanor refers to many studies worldwide, showing a correlation between rising levels of education for women and falling birthrates. She writes that 'No Kids' has been the panacea for an increasing number of 'ambitious' women who don't want to give up their careers. Frazzled, stressed and guilty at both ends, they don't fancy the lot of the working mother who has to move sideways, struggling to perform dual roles. The author admits that giving birth to new life is a gift, but she ends with a confession that it also requires a sacrifice.

Point taken Madam Eleanor, but isn't the charge of motherhood special and paramount enough to be sanctified with sincere sacrifices? Yes, of course, it is! And then, only a woman can offer sacrifices for being a mother since motherhood is a *sine qua non* of her existence.

Ironically, the concept of motherhood is facing a queer onslaught. It's in for a radical revision nowadays. The news that *Male couples could conceive a child,* is a grim pointer. Confronted with the rapid social change and the staggering implications of the biological sciences, the world is perhaps in for a doom. Our successful control over genetics or eugenics depends upon our dealing with it as it is, and not in attempting to reshuffle and mutate it to suit man-made fancies. The 'revolutionary' concept of *Equality* between sexes clashes with an extremely important fact: that biologically both sexes are not equal and are not meant to shoulder an equal amount of burden. For who can deny the plain fact that no male can ever be a good mother and that there is no female who can be a better father.

The fact remains that deviations from Nature have never been able to achieve any positive gain. They, in turn, entail the loss of desirable features of human existence. The correct place for any thing is that assigned to it by Nature. Any bid to displace or re-orient it inevitably leads to a number of moral complications, as has been witnessed in the form of homosexuality, lesbianism, AIDS and surrogacy.

It's not yet too late for those waging a war against Nature to accept the principles of Nature and save themselves from certain doom. Franklin Roosevelt, the late President of America once said of the French—"This beautiful nation is committing suicide. A people whose women are not convinced that there is nothing more beautiful for them than to be a good wife and mother, is a people who have serious reasons to be alarmed of its future."

Perhaps it would be the Apocalypse, having more coffins than cradles, as those whose break the fundamental laws of life, simply vanish in the thin air. This can be the ultimate predicament. More so, when the stupendous hand that used to rock the cradle, now struggles for nothing but the self-aggrandizement. Still and all, we would say – *'Che huew kahn Vuchum nai Wafadaar Mouji'(No one I found as loyal as you, mother)*

Lala Ded : Communicator Par Excellence?

We *live in* communication rather than *outside* communication and use communication for our own purposes. That's why the patterns of social communication constitute the world as we know. It is a primary social process where communication becomes the locus of forces through which persons create and manage *Social Reality* which includes – Concept of Self, Concept of Community and Concept of Cultures.

Through communication we create concepts of self: Who we are? We create relationships within the community and build institutions. We communicate and act together to create and recreate community relationships. Relationships exist and are managed within a culture. That's why human communication notion is not always getting the accuracy of transmission but of social-reality creation.

From the communication perspective, human actions are seen as the process by which persons collectively maintain *social reality*. Human beings simultaneously live in a symbolic universe (social reality) and are engaged in sequences of interactions with their environment and other people. They actively strive to create coherent messages drawing from the resources of their social reality and from the practices in which they are engaged with others.

The primary model that supports such communication process is-

SOURCE →MESSAGE→CHANNEL→RECEIVER

The source of a message is the central person doing the communicating. Lal Ded as a source is shrouded in myth, miracle, and legend. Was she a 'Saint or Social Rebel'- the queries are bamboozling.

Poorly researched and not well documented, her life description lacks veracity. Given the socio-politic and cultural milieu of her times, people perceived her differently. Chroniclers and historians of repute are silent about her. A group of scholars project her as an ascetic, *sadhvi, yogini* adept at a form of meditation (*Kundalini Yoga / Trikashastra*) and a profound exponent of *Shavism* in Kashmir, while others opine that she was a mystic, iconoclast, poetess, a social-rebel whose exclusive art of conveying message through a peculiar form of poetry earned her a mass-appeal. This appeal was reflection of her pristine verses.

In his book *Kashmir's Transition to Islam-The Role of Muslim Rishis*, Prof. M.Ishaq Khan writes that in an 'environment which was undoubtedly exposed to Islamic influences centuries before the establishment of the Muslim Sultanate', Lal Ded had three options before her—

To embrace Islam
To reform Hindu society
To revolt against caste-ridden social order

The first option cannot be taken for lack of substantial evidence. Her conversion is not credibly established from history, however the influence of mysticism, Sufis and Islamic scholars of great standing is felt in her poetry.

The second one, as per Prof. Khan, flounders on the bedrock of her seminal historical role which speaks more of her association with Islam than with Shavism. The last option is established by her message that was replete with dissent against 'social and spiritual pretensions of the Brahmans' of the time.

Lal Ded is the first woman mystic to preach medieval mysticism in Kashmiri poetry. Her messages in the form of *Vaaks* were a forceful expression of incisive metaphors, riddles and semantic symbols. Her message deprecated and disgraced the established organized and instutionalized religion of the time by attempting to present a simplistic, countryside – interpretation of Man, Supernatural and their 'possible confluence' by practicing asceticism and penance as a result of engaging in extreme forms of meditation and yoga.

Though down the ages, folklore and fable has filled in the unanswered questions and queries about her person and life, but the concept of God and religion in her message remains obscure. In the face of her *vaaks* being conspicuously emphatic on issues that demanded tremendous physical toil and dedication for attaining purity of self by total renunciation of world, society and peoples, obscurity in some key aspects is reflective as well as amazing.

Her public and popular demeanor notwithstanding, the contemporary proponents of Islam- who were in the process of gaining foothold at the time treated her poetry as a disguised support whilst people of her community thought of her as a savior in the backdrop of ragging casteism and sectarianism perpetuated by the their religion.

The medium used by Lal Ded was *Oral word*, in the form of Kashmiri Language. Being a language that had people could associate and identify with, her message cut through the cords of common masses who were reeling under transitory but equally historical situations.

Common masses of the time were her target audience. Her denunciation of casteism, peculiar yet simplistic form of poetry, her mental synchronism and amiability with *Rishis* and *Sufis* were the main factors for her mass-appeal. It was an *Age of Social Ferment,* upheavals of lasting magnitude were making inroads.

Given the *Synchronic* and *Diachronic* perspective of communication, the efficacy of Lal Ded's message raises lot f skepticism in the contemporary era. That her message was effective because of its temporal dimensions is a moot point. Putting her in today's settings will not only alter her status as a *Communicato*r but will surely place her message on the testing crucible of *Rationalism* that has overtook most of the present generation.

For a student like me, the following *Vaak* of Lal Ded raises certain questions-

"That transcendental- self may assume the names of Shiva, Vishnu, Buddha or Brahma; I am concerned only With their efficacy in cutting asunder my worldly affections, which might be accomplished by any one of these."

For me, a rep of my generation, *Shiva, Vishnu, Buddha or Brahma* whisk many qualms, forcing to break certain shibboleths that have been fed into my mind over years.

Discerning spiritual vision of Lal Ded, is the indispensable requirement of our times. Separating her genuine outpourings from the spurious interpolations can be taken over by objective research and study, thus freeing Lal Ded from the trappings of many myths and legends. To reconstruct her image in the light of authentic fact and looking at her as a poet who gave voice to women seems mandatory before going into any kind of intellectual or literary debate about figures like Lal Ded who have been the victims of misinterpretation and misrepresentation at the hands of our 'pseudo-historians.'

The Life Pullers

Henry Thoreau, the nineteenth century writer, naturalist and philosopher, said: 'It is something to be able to paint a particular picture, or to carve a statue, and so to make a few objects beautiful; but it is far more glorious to carve and paint the very atmosphere and medium through which we look….To affect the quality of the day—that is the highest of arts.'

Henry tried to remind us that great art is not restricted to painting, music, sculpture or writing. There is an art of living, too. He makes us think of people who through the nobility of their lives, affected the "quality of the day". There is no limit to the number of such artists. It includes the countless obscure, good people who quietly affect the lives of those around them, without even being aware they are doing it, wining no commendation, and even expecting none.

Perhaps it's essential for everybody to have known such people who change the quality of the day at one time or another. They knock at the door of a room in a dark hour, a room without hope, or merely at a moment when we are lonely and lost. Their shadows say little, they say littlest. But the shining quality of inseparable goodness radiates from them; it illuminates everything, subtly and silently. They give us a reason to live, a fragile reason amidst a frigid reality. They give us a wave of energy to ride on, urge us to develop all that we are or can be. Due to them, we grow and are renewed.

A woman needs a little more, always, in everything. For her, it's impossible to go without a support, especially when she as a mature woman glimpses into a mirror that provides a moment of truth. She searches not only her changing face but the very likeness of her soul. The looking glass may not be an actual mirror, but a reflection of hers as she sees it. The more such a woman studies herself, the less she knows how she really looks. And here's the reason. She is victimized by the images around her – her lives of the so-called most beautiful and successful women in the world! She measures herself against these prototypes, and subconsciously begins to identify herself with them. She also falls into the habit of studying herself only from her 'best' angles – seeing, and yet not seeing, herself. As a result, she is convinced that she is much better than she really is. She expects everybody to share this fiction. Shown her picture, she simply doesn't recognize herself.

Her pursuits prove as meaningless answers to the real problems; the rediscovery of a woman's identity as a person with a contribution to make to herself, her home, her community. To change her image, she forgets to change her life. She forgets that she has to take her place as a *contributor*. There are thousand ways to achieve such purpose: art, science, profession (at home or in her community), teaching, counseling, guiding—to name a few.

There are many instances which can hold a mirror up to a woman's nature and present her with a new, more beautiful image of herself. There is a difference in the face she wears for the world, and in the depths of her being. Undoubtedly, a woman can't do it on her own. She needs someone to support and guide her, for it is the profound and painful fact of life that people heal, and people destroy. We help or hinder one another, by holding out our hand or holding it back, by summoning one another to be and grow, or to surrender and retreat.

Recall the poet Robert Browning. He literally invited Elizabeth Barret to live. Elizabeth's mother had died when she was very young and her father assumed a despotic, tyrannical rule over the family. Frail most of her life, Elizabeth eventually became a chair-bound invalid, accepting the doctor's verdict that she had "consumption", clinging to symptoms that defeated her talent for living. Perhaps she unconsciously wanted it so; being ill, she got special care and comparative freedom from her father's rages. When she was nearly 40, she met Robert Browning. Overcoming her fears, he swept her into marriage, dismissing her symptoms as so many cobwebs. At 41, she travelled extensively; at 43, she bore a perfectly healthy child. For the rest of her life, she wrote highly acclaimed poetry that could come only from a vital person.

The splendid people like Browning save us from our skepticism, our weariness, and our disinterest. They overcome the apathy which seizes us. They make everything real—joy, tragedy, and even death. They are the kindlers of life: calling us to be kicking and alive.

Of course, no one is perfect. But everyone possesses some good, even lovable traits. The lovability needs to be recognized and fed. Author Lewis Caroll wrote a fantasy about a lock that keeps running around in distress crying – *'I'm looking for someone to unlock me.'* This story sounds strange, but we need to hold this picture in our minds. Many people need a key to unlock them. They need someone who will bring out all the shining goodness that is locked within them, and encourage it to grow. For growth is the very insignia of every living creature, the heart of the life process: the life that is actually a growing tree, not a statue.

Our times are perilous, true. But they are also open ended, stimulating, and full of possibility. We can live when we are true to ourselves, authentic in our feelings, and responsive to our convictions. We can live when we love, when we are involved in the lives of others, when we are committed and concerned. We can live when we build and create, hope and help, suffer and rejoice.

Woman is instrumental in the working of nature. Her presence makes a difference; and it surely makes a *big* difference when she knows the art of living or knows to learn it gracefully from someone else. She cannot live against her type, which is after all, her essence. A woman who assumes a type becomes artificial. She becomes stiff, kills the dream, paralyses the hope, and cripples the joy. Life shrivels under her skeptical gaze, achievements dwindle, confidence vanishes and fear takes its place. Such a woman does no good, neither to herself nor to others. She becomes good-for-nothing, and nothing else.

White House Epics

The Hollywood movie *Kisses for My President* tells the story of a married American woman who is elected as the US President. She immediately gets in a family way and finds herself faced with so many problems that she decides to resign from the office. Unable to carry on the dual responsibilities, she finally quits.

However, in reality, there was a woman in America who stoutly ran the whole affairs of government, though un-officially. For six weeks after President Woodrow Wilson suffered an incapacitating stroke, his wife Edith Wilson ran the USA, and simultaneously sustained her husband with her love and courage.

President Wilson's agony took birth in Colorado (1919), after three weeks of an exhausting whistle-stop campaign to commit America to join the League of Nations. He suffered head pains so excruciating that he yielded to his wife's pleas, cancelled the rest of his speaking engagements and returned to the White House. A fall in the bathroom further aggravated his state, leading to a cerebral thrombosis. He got paralysed.

For two days, the President hovered between life and death. Specialists examined him, and a vague medical bulletin calling Wilson "a very sick man" only fuelled the rumours swirling through Washington. As per one, the President was a victim of syphilis contracted from a Fresh prostitute. Another pictured him as a mad man, citing bars on a White House window as proof that he was incarcerated. The fact that a specialist in nervous and mental disease had been called, was considered enough for the President being declared insane. However, the specialist found the President's brain as clear as ever and there was every reason to think that recovery was possible if President was left undisturbed for a certain span of time.

Edith Wilson had shared the ordeal of the Presidency with Woodrow Wilson to an extra-ordinary degree. Woodrow was a loner who ran the nation's highest office almost single handed, often preferring to type out his own messages and memoranda, talking over his ideas with those close to him, and no one was closer than his wife. As such, Edith was well-acquainted with all that used to transpire in the white House. For nearly six weeks, she ran the USA – dealing not only with blasts of criticism from Congress, the cabinet and the newspapers but with the ailing President himself. Grimly sticking to no-visitor policy, she hardly allowed anybody to see Woodrow. Only once during this period, Senator Gilbert Hitchcock conveyed to President that unless he changed his position, they had no hope of mustering the necessary two third vote for the League of Nations. For the moment, Edith wavered and thought that a compromised, but ratified, treaty can give her husband the peace she wanted so much for him. She walked to her husband's bedside and said – "Woodrow, for my sake, won't you accept these reservations and get this awful thing settled?" The reply in return silenced her – "Better a thousand times to go down fighting than to dip your colours to *dishonourable compromises*". The fight for the treaty and the League of Nations ran forever into a rough weather. Woodrow's intransigence infuriated his enemies in the Senate, and the treaty, the dream for which Edith and Woodrow had sacrificed so much, went down to a crushing defeat. Their precious dream, no doubt, got shattered into smithereens but their honour and honesty didn't. And this was the most admirable consolation for them.

During the last year of term, Woodrow remained a crippled President– with Edith his closest adviser and constant companion. After leaving the White House, she gave him the same devotion and care until his death in 1924. She was American's first undeclared Woman President, but more than that, the valiant woman who epitomized strength, courage, and pristine love.

So was Madam Eleanor Roosevelt, wife of another American President Franklin Roosevelt. She was not the best lady, but she was voted the most admired woman in America. Lacking seductive looks and shameless candour, she was fortunately unremarkable but painfully reticent for most of her life. Nonetheless, it's she who was named the "First Lady of the Western World". She was berated for interfering into affairs of state, but she was the eyes and ears of President. She was raised in a wealthy, cloistered society that knew none except its own, but she spent her life as a champion of the underdog. She was a woman ahead of her time: warm, loving, sincere, kind, strong, disciplined. A very human person who used her talents and position to help bring about much needed social change. She wrote her *My Day* column from 1935 until shortly before her death in 1962. The column was 500 words long and appeared six days a week. The only days it wasn't published were the four days after President Roosevelt's death. Whether she was at home in the White House, visiting the troops in the South Pacific, working at the UN in Paris, the column was written and dispatched to the syndicate that distributed it to many newspapers in which it ran. The columns touched on every imaginable topic, both controversial and mundane. Whatever the subject, Eleanor put her heart, soul and thought into it. That she wrote each column in about an hour is almost as amazing as the woman herself. Once she wrote in the columns of *My Day*– "My life is so arranged that I can live on whatever I have and have not. Never letting my cherished principles and limitations go away I shall live differently. And living differently does not mean bogging down meekly before the brute forces of time and life. The horizons are wide open, the sky is calling me. The ethereal euphonies are many. I shall live differently to fly away and catch them, leaving behind all nihilities." And as it was, her days obviously proved different and exquisite for she was a mettlesome woman worth her salt.

Similarly, Hillary Clinton, the better half of former President of USA, is a woman who adopted the name of an emotional moron like Clinton, gave up her lawyer job, dressed to soften her image and baked cookies. An erstwhile rabid feminist, she displayed the first-rate sensibility during the crisis that zipped down her idealized husband's 'high profile' reputation into a shit bag. Following ardently the three M's – marriage, monogamy and the missionary position – of a typical Christian lady, she bravely withstood the billows of so-called sexual Mc Carthyism that virtually lashed her marital world. Now in a prestigious office, she has penned down her ruminative biography An *Invitation from the White House*, giving vivid details of her days at the sheeny synagogue of American democracy, besides her fidelity to an 'adventurous' hubby who will be christened as the smart sugar-daddy of American history.

Apparently, the First Ladies occupying the White House far exceeded their husbands in almost all respects, even as they tactfully avoided the limelight. Almost all of them, even as this can't be generalized, stood behind their husbands in thick and thin, quite unexpectedly. This strangely happened in a society where so-called family values are given least priority, religion is a personal affair, morality is a relative term, and licentiousness and promiscuity are so banal to be termed as 'normal'.

IB-intellectuals

Four 'intellectuals' were outlining policies for world salvation.

One said-'Now if we could get rid of all the whiskey, we could have a better world'. Another said-'And if we could get rid of all profanity, we would have a better world'.

The third remarked-'If we could get rid of these and all other sins that plague mankind, then we would have a millennium'.

Whereupon the fourth observed-'Yes, and then we'd have that to put up with'.

Such a generic cohort of 'intellectuals' exists everywhere. In fact, the nouveau-intellectual has sneaked into the lime light. He is the product of idiot-box (IB). We can term him as IB-intellectual. You can also call him tele-intellectual. He could be anyone and anything. He has to do nothing but comply with the 'intellectual Vogue'. Yes, he has to remember certain words, writers and big guns to mention. Name-dropping is, actually, his forte.

Information explosion, Global village, Facebook, Twitter, 3G, Bluetooth and the biggest buzzword- modernity.

Murdoch, Turner, Madonna, Justin Beeber, Yanni, Aby Baby and Rab Rab Kardi Daler Mehndi.

Sydney Sheldon, Rushide, Vikram Seth, Khuswant Singh, Shobha De and of course, larger-than-life-size Arundhati Roy.

Ideas are on parade and he, the IB-intellectual has to whip up them anyway. He cannot afford oblivion and that too, in this, age of 'uncle-chips-intellectuality' where he is cashed and carried away by advertisers, and ultimately reduced to a copycat.

The other day, after a long time, I boarded a local bus from home to city centre. Two young boys, rather hunks, with earrings in one ear and shoulder-length hair, were seated in front of me. Their tongues were wagging throughout the journey. Perhaps trying to fret, strut and attract attention as per the 'intellectual vogue'.

While their 'rhetorical' conversation was on, they often clasped their hands and shouted unnecessarily in unison-'America is happening, man'. All passengers were staring them with surprise. For the moment, I felt I am among New Yorkers. But instantly, I sensed something happening. No, not America!! It was a noisy scuffle between the bus conductor and these two hip-hop guys over something trivial. The big fight was about worn out currency note. The cloak of hi-fi intellectual vogue dropped down abruptly, and both the 'Yankees' hurled obscene Kashmiri invectives on the artless bus conductor. Back to roots, no more America—I thought with a chuckle.

The event made me comprehend the difference between intellection and imitation. Through former, there is no room for cross aping of any damn thing that is beamed out deliberately from idiot-box. Real intellect resents superficiality, and anything that gives it dingbats. 'Uncle-chips intellectuality' is, in fact, no intellectuality. It is simply the worst form of mental slavery. Slavery to alien cultures and ideas while throttling your own socio-cultural ethos. And then, such imported things do not help in obliterating your inherent flaws even if you adopt it out and out. You can only mask them.

There is no point in abhorring IB-intellectuals. May be they all come out as real intellectuals someday! Who knows. Nothing can be ruled out. After all, this is an Age of Surprises! Couch potatoes nowadays are more 'knowledgeable' than many of our 'scholars'. But what should be taken care of is that we must try to resist the attempts designed to partition our intellect and psyche between surrealism and realism. Idiot box should not be allowed to become a weapon of mass-indoctrination. Especially our Gen-next, which is hooked up in wrong interpretation of modernity and whose beliefs are getting moulded by the kind and level of their exposure towards technology.

Possibly our homes alone can chip in to break this inflating vortex. The ambience at family unit is vital in shaping up the perspectives. More significantly when our educational institutions are bereft of any sensitivity for value education and our kids have no option but to enter into these grand gates of bewilderment, not real knowledge.

In fact, time already seems to have arrived where classroom is losing meaning and relevance because of overriding exposure towards gizmos and gadgets. Knowledge is changing its contours and learners are walking and talking IB. There is no room for the mind to be used creatively.

And that's why even proper definition of Intellectual has undergone metamorphosis and you have so many self-styled 'enlightened intellectuals' around to wag their tongues and tails every now and then.

To quote Mark Twain-"The fact that man knows right from wrong proves his intellectual superiority to other creatures; but the fact that he can do wrong proves his moral inferiority to any creature that cannot".

False theme song

'If life can have a *theme song*—and I believe that every worthwhile one has—mine is best expressed in one word: Individualism'.

This is Ayn Rand speaking. Known as the 20th century's most controversial novelist-philosophers, she was born to a Jewish family in 1905 czarist Russia. In her autobiographical notes, she mentions of herself at the age of nine when she decided to make fiction-writing her career. Walter Scott and Victor Hugo inspired her. When 21, she left for Hollywood to become a screenwriter. However, she had to opt for various other jobs until her first novel *We The Living* was published. She, through her fictional characters, formulated "a philosophy for living on earth" and gave it the name of *Objectivism*. The best one line summary of her *Objectivism* comes from Ayn Rand's own lips: "My philosophy, in essence, is the concept of man as a heroic being, with his own happiness as the moral purpose of his life, with productive achievement as his noblest activity and reason as his only absolute" (appendix to *Atlas Shrugged*).

Her novel *The Fountainhead* brought her laurels beyond expectation. The depiction of its main character Howard Roark, a hero, was the paramount purpose of her writing— "the ideal man, man as he could be and ought to be." Strange and yet alluring is the case of Howard Roark, the competent architect but a conceited and an utterly selfish creature. Rand writes of him, "Born without any 'religious brain centre', he does not understand and even conceive of the instinct for bowing and submission...The world has no painful surprise for him.... He does not suffer, because he does not believe in suffering. Defeat or disappointment are merely a part of the battle. Nothing can really touch him. He is concerned only with what he does. Not how he feels."

So, Howard is a typical phlegmatic person who lives just for his own self alone. This is evident from a single line from Howard to a question of Toohey (a humanitarian in the novel) as to what he thinks of him. Howard answers snobbishly–"But I don't think of you."

Howard Roark is the simon-pure spokesperson of Rand, living for his own sake, rejecting every form of human sacrifice. Anti-altruistic, Rand wants him work for his own self-interest. However, in the process, Rand unwittingly, makes her hero lose many of life's little but precious possessions.

In fact, in many of her novels, there are instances where Rand has tactfully and, of course, artistically overpowered even genuinely natural emotions by the iron-rod of reason. Upholding the killing of emotions altogether as a *magnum opus,* she has lend a psychologically abnormal and unwontedly obdurate colour to her great literary style. That life requires not only the gaining of values but sometimes even their loss; not only victory but sometimes even failures; not only honour but sometimes even humiliation; and not only self-preservation but sometimes even self-sacrifice—is a simple logic perhaps missed too miserably by a woman of Ms Rand's caliber. Moreover, that there is a hell of difference between Ego and Egoism, also continued to elude Rand. The former never hinders one to live and feel for others, whilst the latter always dictates one to shove nonchalantly through others, living and dying only for one's own life and world. And this perhaps is no big deal, and does not involve any 'extra-ordinary' mettle as propounded by Rand. Actually, when you sacrifice and still sing; when you suffer and still smile; when you die and still live—that's dynamism, that's gallantry. Ego makes you humbly humane; egoism renders you stolidly brute. Rand missed the point. However, she unreservedly succeeded in creating many Howard minds around, handing over to them a false theme song for life.

Needless to say, the prolific and immensely creative writings of Ayn Rand notwithstanding, her literary contributions are undoubtedly remarkable. Nonetheless, the underlying philosophy of her all works and its un-naturalness take much sheen away from her, though millions wade through her masterpieces even today. There is 'Ayn Rand Institute' in US, meant for studying and propagating her philosophy.

The bottomline that her *Objectivism* was nothing but yet another add-on in the junkyard of human engineered inefficacious isms, doctrines, philosophies and ideological aberrations, we suppose, is not outrightly incorrect for if human reason has been raised to the level of God by Ayn Rand, is it surprising that ever-increasing cynicism, injustice and bitterness on earth are the natural fruits, once the gods fail? Perhaps, not. The world today is an eye-opener.

She is on street

The street protests in the valley send many messages across. From fervent political overtones to stanch posturing of public, events have really opened up an interesting mosaic.

The most appealing, from the female viewpoint, was the breaking of certain old socio-political modes. Women in Kashmir vehemently participate in the political activism, breaking away from the tradition. Out on street, they make their angry minds felt. It was a path-breaking moment. A very rare sight. Pelting stones and running to the pace, they were fairly expressive of their collective concern.

Was it just a knee-jerk reaction or blazing trails for women in the future? The answers can be many based on speckled interpretations. This behaviour, the first of its kind in the political history of Kashmir, can be viewed as a slice of allied response to a particular situation. Given the mob dynamics, it can be an upshot of frenzy that overtook all and sundry. It was interesting to see involvement of woman as a whole in the field of public affairs.

Secondly, it may be an indication of the level of discomfort and distress that woman here has reached to. The two decade turmoil has brought her on the front line of clash. Over these years, a kind of support system has been created naturally, where old problems are analyzed in new ways, new possibilities have opened up, and individual change has got transformed into collective change.

There has been a change in her self-image. She is perhaps liberated from her existing perception of herself as a 'weak' and 'limited' being. She has realized that no amount of external interventions, whether in the form of resource access or economic power, will enable her to challenge existing power equations in society.

Woman of Kashmir have started to analyze and critique independently. She has exercised an '*informed choice*' within a diminishing framework of options available. Within the menu of known or experienced possibilities of previous years of tumult, she has discovered a new leeway or option to express herself. Her ability to assert, speaking out and acting on oppressive practices and injustices have burst in the street. Perhaps the agony and affliction she borne out as a central member of society, has made her move in the centrestage of political arena.

However, for certain quarters it seemed that women in Kashmir are unintentionally developing and emerging as a group of "lawbreakers", though many of the analysts of public-thought justify the aggressive behaviour, adding that breaking a 'law' which does not represent the will of the majority is warranted.

The other argument purported in this regard is the 'letdown' of men who have been the worst targets of political resistance. But the same does not hold much water given the brutal magnitude of collective brunt faced by the people over here.

The belligerent behaviour can even be interpreted as a consequence of betrayal wreaked by incessant political gimmickry. There is a flashpoint in every situation that goes chronic, and maybe woman of Kashmir has reached up to it as an added politically conscious being.

No doubt, generalizations don't move beyond a limit in abnormal circumstances. Thing and events continuously morph the public perception and opinion. In five or ten year's time to come, woman of Kashmir may locate herself in an entirely different paradigm. Her role in political activism will socially legitimize her leverage to claim a seat as a stakeholder in any kind of political process.

This seems to suggest that the course of *actual empowerment* is gradually chipping in. The progression that begins in the mind, from woman's consciousness: from her very beliefs about herself and her rights, capacities, and potential; from her self-image and awareness of how gender as well as other socio-economic and political forces are acting on her; from her breaking free of the stereotypes; from recognizing her strengths, her knowledge, intelligence and skills; above all, from believing in her innate right to dignity and justice, and realizing that it is **she**, along with her sisters, who must assert that right, for no one who holds power will give it away easily and willingly.

Breathing in turmoil

Hermione Granger, Harry Potter's daring and dedicated companion in his battle against evil is not simply an average 11 year old girl. She is a bright student at Hogwarts School, besides a modern manifestation of an ancient archetype, embodied by Athena, the Greek goddess of wisdom and war. Harry Potter seeks Hermione's help in his fight with his rival, the evil wizard Lord Voldemort. The whole story has a counsel. Trailing Hermione's way, women can learn to interlace vigor and vulnerability, intellect and imagination, and draw in compassion and clemency into the male domain. Which is what so many women can hardly do even if they carry on against all odds, especially in a conflict torn area.

The hardships of equally fearless but even more audacious women who have been battling against real life drama would tax even British writer JK Rowling's prolific imagination. She cannot put them up in history as 'anecdotal evidence' for her view of the world because it would be naïve for her to visualize a woman sitting on a roadside protesting the arrest of her son or husband. Or wailing over his baffling disappearance. That she can be a young widow struggling for some loaves of bread, holding up a deportment of self-respect close to her wounds is something fiction-sellers don't typically make out. When woes plague her, intellect no longer pacifies. Big talks, high ideals, tall values: everything boils down to mere continued existence, and that too for little accessions.

The scene of a woman walking through desolate fields with a water pitcher or stack of firewood over her head and nozzle of gun overseeing her from the bunker at the hilltop—it surely symbolizes nerve. But at what kind of a cost? It is harrowing insecurity. It is suffering uncertainty.

The man at duty stopping her vehicle, getting her down, frisking all her belongings, questioning her credentials—her identity is lost in the humiliating crossfire. Many historical factoids can be cited, but they are just window-dressing People only write about gallantry but she glugs it down practically. And she is quite oblivious of it.

From illiterate rustic to qualified urbanite, her rank is alike. Her plight is identical. She is no exceptional entity barring her knack to contain all predicaments. She has faced the storm in various parts of world, she tastes it in Kashmir. The continuum of violence is equally distressing and alarming.

What happened in neighboring Afghanistan makes a strangely interesting story. Before the skirmishing that has rocked the area for the last so many decades, women played an essential role in Afghan society, accounting for 70 per cent of the country's teachers, 50 per cent of its civil servants and 40 per cent of its doctors *(Arianna Huffington's columns: Arianna Online)*. For the situation prevailing, Taliban are barely to be blamed knowing what happened in the early 90's with Burhanuddin Rabbani clinging to power. During his four years as president of Afghanistan from 1992 until 1996, the forces used systematic rape, abduction, enslavement and murder to effect the complete and utter humiliation of Afghan women. Surprisingly, the crime against women dwindled during Taliban regime!

Back home, things might not seem that appalling. But with likes of Shopian tragedy in the backyard, things aren't even un-ghastly. Instances of atrocities, dishonor and ignominy are concrete truths. The level of discomfort and distress that woman here has reached to is sickening. The two decade turmoil has brought her on the front line of clash. Over these years, a kind of support system has been created naturally, where old problems are analyzed in new ways, new possibilities have opened up, and individual change has got transformed into a collective change.

There has been a change in her self-image, as well. She is perhaps liberated from her existing perception of herself as a 'weak' and 'limited' being. She has realized that no amount of external interventions, whether in the form of resource access or economic power, will enable her to challenge the existing power equations in society.

Woman of Kashmir has started to analyze and critique independently. She has exercised an '*informed choice*' within a diminishing framework of options available. Within the menu of known or experienced possibilities of previous years of tumult, she has discovered a new leeway or option to express herself. Her ability to assert, speaking out and acting on oppressive practices and injustices have burst in the street, too. Perhaps the agony and affliction she borne out as a central member of society, has made her move in the centre stage of political arena.

Needless to say, evil is hard to defeat, even in the magical realm of Hogwarts. It would have been imprudent for Harry Potter to enter the deadly dungeon without Hermione and her vast knowledge by his side. Likewise, it would be silly to move forward in the crusade against disgrace, and the hard work of rebuilding certain values, if more than half of the population of world is not allowed to join this fray and live a dignified life, especially in any turbulent territory.

Shame on us!

Romana, a teenage girl from Srinagar, the summer capital of Kashmir, was put to death by a delinquent youth who went completely gaga with a hidden beast in him and crushed down Romana lethally. This time the accused are behind the bars, but the reports insinuate that the scuffle for getting bail is already in.

The violence against women in Kashmir is now reaching to a disgusting point, something which was quite unthinkable some years a ago. The debilitating experience of physical, psychological, and/or sexual abuse is getting rampant. The crime record is displaying an alarming rise.

Every female in Kashmir has no immunity against this dastard violence. The victims have been illiterate village girls to educated urban daughters who are strangulated to death. From the mysterious murder of a young girl in posh Hyderpora area in 2008, to the recent killing of Farzana in downtown city, there is a chilling shame for all of us.

There is nothing private about our shamelessness. Though many of us, as a part of dead civil society are witness to lot of such happenings around, we are too cowardly to react and register our annoyance. For bogus cultural reasons, we tend to accept the idea that it's socially odd for to raise our voice against crime towards women. For many of men here, woman is still no more than a piece of property. Absurd!

In the upper and middle classes, where privacy of both emotions and acts is maintained, family members quite conveniently feign ignorance of the violence their womenfolk face within and without. The usual reaction is that it's a "personal" problem. Consequently, when it becomes a daily problem, it's ignored.

Equally astonishing is the attitude of the families of the victims who express meek helplessness. Though their reticence does not justify the violence, they nonetheless silently endure it for other reasons. Fear of social stigma being the one. It seals their expression.

The efforts of Police in busting such incidents are commendable, but there is much more to do beyond just cracking the murders in a Hitchcock style. The follow-up of cases in a just manner, without succumbing to any influence, is an immediate requirement. Money, high contacts and hush up mentality should not lure them. Moral policing, of course, cannot be their domain, especially when the State is in a conflict mode.

The government in Kashmir is not noticeable anywhere. Its anarchy all around! Our rulers and ministers are invisible *maharajas*, least concerned about their *praja*. Stunningly, when even morally tainted ones are also our masters, it would be naïve to anticipate any meaningful intervention from them.

The role of *Imaams* in creating deep sensitization about moral values and respect for dignity of women is dismal. By the same token, the proper guidance and counseling of women is also missing. There is no alarm around to venture on moral crusade even as more killings result from moral waywardness and social aberrations. The warranted moral panic is absent. The strange nonchalance is turning criminal. The pulpits are mute about the whole scenario.

The religious institutions and leaders of our society are meshed up in the network of amassing power and money to expand and propagate their organizational/individual versions of religion. The mushroom growth of palatial mosques, *darsgahs* and *darul-alooms* has been their priority. It hasn't stopped there, they are 'dedicated' to construct global universities and mega institutions, least bothered about the moral rot set in the society. The dabbling in politics is far imperative to them than dabbling in moral affairs of this misguided society. Shocking!

In fact, politics has overshadowed everything in Kashmir. Obsession with politics is becoming our manna. We are putting everything at altar, even our morality for recompense in politics. We don't seem to be concerned with the rape of our womenfolk; we are concerned with rape being used as a war weapon. We don't shy away to reap political mileage out of crime against our women: human rights violations are a pliable way out. Our men—whether leaders, politicians, officials, teachers, husbands, fathers or brothers—have failed miserably to salvage women from any kind of menace. Even as *Azaadi* is so critical to this diseased society, the women of this nation are increasingly getting fettered by aggression from all quarters and sources.

We are yet to recognize that woman is a God's gift: A fragile soul with strong resilience to wade through thin and thick, and make mankind forget the wretchedness of survival by lending a hand to saunter through the dark alleyways of life smilingly.

Doesn't such a hand need to be cared, protected and not annihilated with impudence?! Let woman of this nation be not another woman who died yesterday at the hands of any man; let she be the hope that survives for all our tomorrows, even amidst worst moral catastrophe.

Allama Iqbal's Feminism

Ik Bulbul Hai Ke Mahve Tarannum Ab Tak,
Is Kay Seene Mai Hai Naghmaon Ka Talatum Ab Tak
(Remains of one nightingale, in its song's raptures lost;
its bosom is full of melodies that are still tempest tossed)

Yes, they are the reflective melodies, full of extra-ordinary sense and thought, effusively composed by none other than Allama Iqbal – the poetic genius of the East.

Allama remains one of the most stimulating and polemical poets of the sub-continent. His mature poetry in Urdu and Persian is great literature endowed with lofty imagination, metaphysical insight, and an almost epigrammatic elucidation of concepts like ego, self, life force, freedom and consciousness. Allama is a challenging poet to read as he seems to straddle different positions with felicity at different times, sometimes even running counter to the convictions and concepts he himself has constructed. And this, perhaps, is nothing new or baffling as far as the vast experience of such men-of-letters is concerned.

For who can deny Allama wasn't a romantic poet by nature, yet his emotional outbursts under few poetic pieces like *Wisaal, Husn-o-Ishq, Nawa-i-Gum* and *Phool Ka Toufa* are replete with various poignant nuances. However, unlike Ghalib, his style at romanticism is highly symbolic and not so limpid. Ghalib's romantic overtones were too intellectual to have a deep emotional quality, albeit he is branded as 'candid romanticist'. His was the self assertive style, implying a negation of everything except the poetic mood and the poetic image. It was a pure aesthetic experience, a visceral glory that was known neither to Ghalib as a lover nor to his beloved, but encompassed both.

Nonetheless, Allama's definition about women transcended beyond poetic flights. It was a well intentioned, well meant and well wrought philosophy. In his famous anthology of lectures *The Reconstruction of Religious Thoughts in Islam,* he admits– "The kind of knowledge that poetic inspiration brings is essentially individual in its character; it is figurative, vague and indefinite. Religion, in its more advanced forms, rises higher than poetry. It moves from individual to society."

So originated the Allama's doctrine about *Wajood-i-Zan,* which surpassed the bitterness of his unstable marital life and overviewed the wider perspective of women amelioration. And of course, he found religious ethos indispensable for the same.

The woman of Allama's thought is a paragon of nobility, vindicated even by the purity of scintillating moon and sheeny constellations—

Ghawah Is Ki Sharafat Pay Hain Mah-o-Parveen...

Vehemently rejecting the idea of 'Women's Lib', he was totally against any kind of ideological fracas that led to the decline in cultural, moral and spiritual values of any society. He believed that when moral depravity and sensual indulgence touch extremes and people turn perverts, the natural consequences leading a nation to total collapse inevitably follow. Antagonistic about free mixing of sexes, which rendered woman frippet, Allama aspired for a community bereft of any 'unadulterated' moral anarchy—

Badh Jata Hai Jab Zauq-i-Nazr Apni Hadoun Sai
Ho Jatay Hai Afkaar Parakanda-o-Abter

The debate of 'feminism' always proved vivisection, and Allama knowing its vanity, often remained low-key even as his verdict was exquisitely unassailable—

Kya Cheez Hai Aarish-o-Keemat Main Zaida
Azaad-i-Niswaa Ki Zamurud Ka Gulobund?

That 'feminism' is an unnatural, artificial, friable and abnormal product of social disintegration, emanating out of outright rejection of all transcendental and absolute spiritual values, was the crux of Iqbal's poetic treatise over woman. He realized that the modern education has robbed woman of her essence and esteem. There was no equivocation about it, and that's why he ordained *Man* as the best custodian of womanhood, the one who alone can rescue her from every kind of storm—

Nishwaaniyat-i-Zan Ka Nigahbaan Hai Fakht Mard
(Man alone is the protector of womanhood)

The poet of the East cannot in anyway be charged of espousing European philosophies as such. He maybe said to belong to the strand of vitalist thought in Europe because of his short sojourn there, which made him sensitive to multiple currents of ideological thought. No doubt, he was greatly impressed by Nietzsche, Whitehead *et al* but Rumi, Ibn-e-Khuldun and other Muslim medieval thinkers equally influenced him. In fact, his exposure to Western capsule-philosophies only served to alert him to the magnitude of their fallacy and ferocity. His poetry, especially the part written about women, leaves one without the slightest doubt as to his clear-cut, unambiguous attitude towards the antediluvian and flunked out western dogmas.

And as far his concept of *Mard-e-Momin* (virtuous men) which derives much of its sustenance and resonance from the

Divine revelations and Prophetic teachings, it serves as the topology of the perfect human being on earth. And woman, obviously, cannot be barred from being the one. After all, she happens to constitute more than half of human-beings on planet earth. The lessons of Ego and secrets of Self are significant and enkindling enough for her too. She can be a *Bulbul (nightingale)* simmering inwardly with hundreds of unsung melodies, or a *Shaheen (Falcon)* dreaming latently to flutter far and far away in the expanse of limitless skies. Else, she can even be the mourning billow that drifts endlessly without destination, flouncing away all travails of time with itself.

The Finest Relation

The first marriage invitation card of this year was lying on the table. On opening it up, the golden words in gold color were striking: *"Holy Prophet (SAW) said, 'By Allah, I am more submissive to Allah and more afraid of Him than you; yet I fast and break my fast, I do sleep and I also marry women. So, he who does not follow my tradition in religion, is not from me (not one of my followers)"*.

This saying of Holy Prophet (SAW) as quoted in *Sahih Bukhari* is usually carried by most of the marriage cards here. However, looking deep, the true essence of this most liked *Sunnah* in the religion of our Holy Prophet (SAW) yet remains to be emphasized. Going far away from the actual fundamental nature of this most loved *Sunnah* of our Holy Prophet (SAW), our marriages are the reflection of our falling into trivialities, and subsequently creating and arguing inconsequential issues regarding them.

One such issue is that of *Mahar* (obligatory bridal money given by the husband to his wife at the time of marriage). As ordained, it is to be given "with a good heart". After the mutual agreement between the bride and the groom, *Mahar* is to be given according to the financial capacity of husband, thereby having no limit. Surprisingly, *Mahar* in Kashmir has been divided into two categories. A very marginal amount is recorded in column of *Mahar* on Nikah papers while as the major amount is documented under the self-made column called as *Thaan* (termed as 'gift'). One wonders if *Mahar* is really given with a good heart, why everything couldn't be registered as *Mahar*. Perhaps, somewhere in the subconscious mind lies a doubt regarding the sustenance/future of this relation, which shapes the provision of taking *Mahar* back in the name of *Thaan*.

The real issue in marriage is the acceptance with love. The day when bride departs for her new home, is enough to remind us of the zenith of sacrifice the bride can offer. She leaves her parents and everyone else with whom she has lived for years, just for one person, her husband. She craves for a place and acceptability in her new home. She starts a new living with people of varying temperaments and personalities. She works hard for the feel of being at home. She pushes herself to be recognized as a family member. She tries to forget her old home because of the love and support she gets there.

Of course, she could succeed only if her husband essentially deliberates on the vital fact that his wife has left everything for him. Endowing his absolute support, selfless love, utmost care, unconditional help, and pure devotion to his wife, he has to be with her in all spheres and seasons of life. And the kind of understanding that emerges out of such bonding is strong enough to overcome any ordeal and come out unshaken.

Undoubtedly, strengthening the connection with Almighty is the best assurance for enduring married life. Holy Prophet (SAW) said, "The best of you are those who are best to their wives". We need to remember that our great Prophet (SAW) used to extend his knee to his wife to assist her up to ride the camel. For which He (SAW) has said, "One would be rewarded for anything that he does seeking the pleasure of Allah even the food that he puts in the mouth of his wife".

While as in return, the wife has to bear in her mind that the man who is her life-partner (*Shareekay hayat*) has not sprouted from stone as a full fleshed prosperous person. There is one mother who has endured him in weaknesses and hardships; battling with death gave birth to him and then happily offered her blood out to him in the form of milk. There is surely a driving force which was his father that has made this man to grow and excel.

Hazrat Ayesha (RA) once asked the Messenger of Allah (SAW), "Who has the greatest rights over a woman?" He said, "Her husband." She asked, "And who has the greatest rights over a man?" He said, "His mother." Thus, a wife has to help her husband in ignoring and winking at the attitudinal flaws of his aged parents, by making him remember how they forgave his every wrong since childhood and endured his imperfections, grooming him into a young man.

She too has to show gratitude to her husband's parents. She cannot be unforgettable of the fact that both of them have sacrificed and slogged all through their life for their son, with a hope that a day would come when they will rejoice their old age with his support and caress, and all else will naturally appear cheerful.

Holy Prophet (SAW) said, "If I were to order anyone to prostrate to anyone else, I would have ordered women to prostrate to their husbands." (*Tirmidhi, 2/314*).

No denying then, a wife has to be wholesomely loyal, enthusiastically obedient, sincerely loving, genuinely caring, and last but not the least, passionately humble towards her husband—the one who follows the matrimonial commandments of Holy Prophet (SAW), and makes himself entitled for the same.

Women of Piety

Supple and strong; tender and tough; mellow and mettlesome—such were the people who personified the existence of Allah practically. They were the paragons of humility and probity. They were the *Companions of Holy Prophet (SAW)*, whose example was inspiring for them. Their lives are the epitome of unlimited sacrifice for the sake of Almighty Allah, the selfless love for His religion and His Prophet. They are the fulgent examples for their successors irrespective of gender, age and class. The women of this era find a special mention in the annals of history, as they carved a niche for themselves by their great deeds that even surpassed men in heroism.

There are glaring examples in the Islamic history that provide insight into the individuality of a woman, which was a basic principle of a religion like Islam. A woman like Fatima (RA), the daughter of Al Khattab, embraced Islam although her brother Umar was still an unbeliever. Similarly, Umm Habiba (RA), the daughter of Abu Sufiyan, adopted Islam though her father was a pagan. When Sufiyan went to Madina, he visited his daughter, then wife of Holy Prophet (SAW). He was about to sit on the Prophet's bed but his daughter did not allow him to do so and rolled up the mattress. Abu Sufiyan, who felt grieved at her attitude, said to her – 'Was it that the mattress is not worthy of me or that I am not worthy thereof". Umm Habiba (RA) curtly replied–"But this is the Prophet's mattress, and you are an impure polytheist. I did not want you to sit on it". Abu Sufiyan felt annoyed and reprimanded her, but his daughter proved strong enough to withstand all that.

Hazrat Zainab (RA), the daughter of Prophet (SAW), was married to her maternal cousin Abu Al-A's bin Al Rabee. She entered the fold of Islam though her husband held on to his original religion. In the battle of Badr, he fell prisoner of war. Zainab (RA), however, offered a ransom for his release. He was, therefore, allowed to go free on the condition that on his return he would let her free. Consequently, when he returned to Mecca, Zainab (RA) migrated to Madina. Influenced by her unflinching conviction, Abu Al-A's later on embraced Islam.

Umm Saleem bint Mahan (RA) was another such lady. She married Malik bin Al Nadir before the advent of Islam and was among the earliest converts to Islam. Her husband, Malik, disapproved of that rather furiously and went to Syria to die there. Similarly, Umm Hani bint Abu Talib (RA) was married to Hubairah bin Amr. She was the daughter of the Prophet's uncle, Abu Talib, and embraced Islam on the occasion of the conquest of Mecca. This change of religion separated her from her husband who fled to Najran.

Hazrat Hawa (RA), the daughter of Yazeed, was yet another woman who acceded to Islam and patiently endured distress and torture at the hands of her husband Qais bin Al Hateem, who was also a well known poet.

Another woman, Hazrat Umm Kulthoom bint Ugba bin Abi Mait embraced Islam even as her whole family was still holding on to its original polytheistic religion. She migrated to Madina while the peace settlement of Hudaibiya was still operative. In fact, she was the first lady to follow the

Prophet (SAW) to Madina. She left Mecca, unaccompanied by anyone.

Harithah bint al Muammil (RA) was a slave girl. She was among the earliest believers in Islam and was one of those women who were severely tortured for their faith. Abu Jahl used to beat her ruthlessly; so did Umar before he embraced Islam. She suffered so much that she lost her sight. The Meccan polytheists used this misfortune as an excuse for stigmatizing her for embracing Islam. They taunted her by saying – "Al Lat and Al Uzza (two deities which the Meccans used to worship in the holy Ka'aba) have rendered you blind". But she, brimmed with the power of her faith, would always say–"They are lying, by the truth of Allah these idols bring no benefit or harm". She ultimately recovered her sight.

Hazrat Sumayah bint Khubat (RA), a martyr, was the mother of Ammer bin Yasir, and was the seventh person to embrace Islam. The Al Mughira clan used to torture her. People used to pass by and witness her being tortured by the side of her son and husband in the hot sands of Mecca. The Prophet (SAW) would console herby saying–"O the Yasirs, bear this suffering patiently, for God has given you the promise of Heaven". She was aged and weak too. She succumbed to the excessive torture and died to become the first person ever to attain martyrdom in Islam.

Muslim women, on the strength of their unshakable personal faith, used to work for the propagation of Islam. Many of them helped to promote the cause of Islam within their respective family circles, through discussion and debate. Arwa bint Abdul Mutallib (RA) was one such lady who used to support the Prophet (SAW) and argued in his favour. Hazrat Um Shuraik (RA) also used to move secretly among the ladies of Quraish to solicit and convert them to

Islam. She had converted many before her missionary work came to light.

Among Muslim ladies were some who invited even their suitors to embrace Islam and made it a pre-condition for marriage. Hazrat Umm Saleem (RA) was one such personality. She said to Abu Talha, who asked her hand in marriage–"By God, one like you cannot be rejected. But you are a polytheist and I am a Muslim woman. It is not at all lawful for me to marry you. If you embrace Islam, I would take that as my dower from you". Anas ibn Maalik is reported to have said that Abu Talha had sent a marriage proposal Umm Saleem (RA) before embracing Islam, and after her reply, he asked to wait till he looked into matter, and went away. Later he returned and proclaimed faith in Islam. Thereupon, Umm Saleem (RA) married him.

Allah's religion was foremost on the minds of Holy Prophet's companions, and women of this age only reflected this thinking. Belonging to the most glorious era of mankind, the women then were fortress of faith binding together the multiple roles of pious mothers, dedicated teachers, loving daughters and obedient wives. The embodiment of righteousness, piety, humility and all that encompassed the best of Muslims in history.

Real Success

Every individual has certain personal handicaps. One's success in life depends first on identifying these, and second, on identifying ways to overcome them, or to succeed in spite of them or because of them.

Pilgrim's progress would probably never have been written had John Bunyan not been imprisoned in the old Bedford jail. Possibly Bunyan had many things in mind that he would have preferred doing—ambitions which would have absorbed his entire life's energies and which would, therefore, have prevented the writing of the now famous allegory.

Bunyan desired to communicate his concepts of Christianity to the world. At first thought, his imprisonment seemed a handicap to the fulfillment of this desire. But he possessed the important quality of finding a way to reach his goal, obstacles notwithstanding. Thus he was forced to use the printed word to accomplish his purpose, and he spent his time in prison preparing the manuscript which became *Pilgrim's progress.*

Looking back on Bunyan's life, we can easily discern that he exerted a far greater influence in the world because of the book he wrote than he would have through any other means. A person of lesser courage, thus confined in jail, might have reasoned that he was justified in abandoning his great life purpose. However, Bunyan found a way, even though it was through hardship. And there lied his real mettle, real worth.

So is it with most successful persons. They have put forth the effort necessary to overcome their handicaps, and perhaps even capitalized on them, using them not as crutches of failure but as aids to success.

Besides, the concept 'success' is itself hard to define. Some measure it in material wealth, others in social accomplishments, and still others in terms of skills like art or science. However, such measures are superficial at best. In the truest sense of the word, the *successful person* is one who lives abundantly: who is happy in every state, who finds satisfactions in life, and who shares his blessings with those around him.

Ironically, not all can achieve the same degree of success. H. G. Wells remarked—'Wealth, notoriety, place, and power are no measures of success whatsoever. The only true measure of success is the ratio between what we might have been, on the one hand, and the thing we have done and the thing we have made of ourselves, on the other'. Success isn't measured, in the long run, by the level of a person's accomplishments, but by the difference between his/her starting point in life and eventual contribution towards his/her society in one or the other way.

This task requires insight: a precious characteristic of the human mind. The person who carries the best prospect of success is the one best acquainted with the strength and weaknesses of his own nature. The quality of being able to look within, to question your inner self, and to make correct and honest evaluations, is what ultimately brings real success to you and saves you from every kind of disaster. The way you react to circumstances—favorably or unfavorably, positively or negatively—it all depends in large measure upon factors of your mind, which principally determine your success or failure, as the case may be.

The life story of Bint Al-Huda is both inspiring and impressive in this regard. Her actual name was Aminah Haider Al-Sadir. She was born in the city of Kadhmain, Baghdad in 1937. Her father, a renowned religious leader, died when she was two years old. She enjoyed the loving care of her mother and two kind brothers. She, due to unfavorable reasons, did not attend any school. Nevertheless, she was well educated at the hands of her two scholar brothers, especially the elder one who recognized her potential. As a teenager, she was a voracious reader who was obsessed with assimilating more and more. It was the time when Western cultural values had dominated the Arab and Muslim countries, and secular systems had started spreading deviation by branding Islam as a 'reactionary' and 'intolerant' religion. The milieu in which Bint Al-Huda grew was surcharged with a lethal bias against Islam, and her personal life too wasn't normal because of domestic problems. However, it was the time when she began writing articles in *Al-Adhwa* magazine, published by the religious ulema in the city of Najaf, Iraq. She was just 20, an innocent mind bubbling with purity of thought. Her writings drew the attention of intellectuals in Najaf, and became flambeaus for awakening a society that was horribly drowning into depths of depravity. Possessing keen insight, she felt the great damage that was being inflicted upon Islam through the deliberate corruption of women. She wrote short stories, later compiled in a form of book entitled *Determination*, and tackled the wrong traditions and notions about her religion by presenting true Islamic concepts, concerning society in general and woman in particular, especially her specific role in a healthy society. Her rising popularity and influence unnerved the then Iraqi Bathist regime, who arrested her along with the elder brother in 1980. Only three days after arrest, both of them were killed in cold blood.

Bint Al-Huda died, but she never passed into oblivion. Success, the simon-pure, licked her life and she lived and died with a purpose.

Whether men or women, successful people are those who face life frankly, accept ups and downs on the same day by accepting facts of life squarely for fighting them out bravely. Such people are the true leading lights of any society; the ones who have the virtual grit to face and evaluate life honestly, without putting up blinkers of superficial and transient popularity on their minds.

Past has to pass

It was an unusual morn. Sunny and crisp-clear for a change. Rhapsodical for a panacea. She settles into a chair in her room. The woozy noise of vehicles and spectacle of the Manhattan skyscrapers outside didn't brother her reverie. Closing the eyes, tuning into the energy in the room, she felt safe, nurtured, as if wrapped in a soft cocoon. Past no longer appeared demonic; the moorings not painful anymore. It wasn't resuscitation; it was resurrection evermore. 'I'm one of you now' – she confessed honestly.

She was India-born, but now she's no more Indian. Adopting a foreign citizenship, she became one among the Americans. India lost nothing for it had never found her. Brain drain is not new to it. And she, as a literary genius, got it early and packed herself off forever.

She's Bharati Mukherjee—the one who bagged the American National Book Critics Circle award (NBCC) in late eighties for her piece of 'realistic' fiction *The Middleman and Other Stories*. The NBCC award is given by the organization of 485 professional book editors and critics from across the country and carries more clout in literary circles in New York—the book capital of the world—than the National Book Awards (sponsored by the publishing industry) or the Pulitzer Prize. Reviewers compared her to greats like John Updike and Vladimir Nabokov, another immigrant, whose *Lolita* was also a paean to America

Catapulted into the same genre as third world prodigies like V S Naipaul and Salman Rushdie, she has had the cheek to proclaim herself an American with no sentimentality or hankering for the 'glorious' Indian heritage. Says she: 'Now America is more real to me than India. India—especially the Hindu religion—has given me a way of looking at things, but India is part of a past that I am proud of but my life is here. I need to belong. America matters to me. It is not that India failed me—rather America transformed me. The letting go of India was very traumatic, but to hang on willy-nilly to an outdated image of the country you've left is to insulate yourself' *(Special Issue, India today)*.

Earlier when Bharati wrote her first novel *The Tiger's Daughter* in 1971, she had a mawkish attitude of projecting realities. *The Tiger's Daughter* was a woman who marries outside her culture and knows that her life is permanently located in the US but whose emotional life is lived in India. At that time, Bharati had two perfectly balanced worlds, drawing on both ambidextrously. She hadn't lost one and hadn't totally immersed herself in the other. She could see the world she had left as intact but she was far away enough to write about it.

The evolution, somehow, occurred. *The Middleman* is about the transition, between two cultures. At ease in both, yet having to negotiate the minefields of being in the middle—being a wheeler-dealer. *The Middleman* is not a book about immigrants so much as a book about the new America. Half the stories are from the White American point of view, half from immigrant points of view –such as Italian, Sri Lankan, Filipino, and Indian. Even as immigrant themes has been the one and only thread that runs firmly through her literary career, Bharati as a petite and vivacious woman has found her true identity with only *The Middleman*. The identity that she claims coincided with her discovery of herself as an American.

Besides, her book broke the ground vis-à-vis the confrontation between the Third World and the First which has escaped the attention of American authors. With motel-owning Patels, grocery-store owning Koreans, illegal West Indian domestics and refugees from Latin America, Middle East and Afghanistan, all pouring into America at an increasing rate, the subject of Bharati's book is something surprisingly contemplative and vital. Making her motley character come alive, she voyages through different minds to almost hear their accents and smell their ambitions. She may not sound nostalgic about her roots—the one she has disowned so calmly—but her writings divulge how she has tracked down her alter ego in various characters who careen through her earthly stories.

Married to Canadian writer Clark Blaise, having two sons, Bharati in her fifties, also teaches writing at Columbia University and Queens college, Determined not to look back, she perhaps is well-aware of the fate that Nirad Chauduri met as an 'unknown Indian' And yet, she empathisizes with her lost roots!

Perhaps it is not so much what people do in this world as their reasons for doing it, which really makes a difference. Sacrifices are not as important as the reasons for which you sacrifice, and then hold no regrets, no remorse.

Bharati did it well. And only few like her can do it that way. She no longer longs for India, for she belongs to America.

Home, a small magic world

Despondency at its worst; poesy at its best. What is it that makes a genius like Ghalib to detest and disown something called *Apna Aashiyanaa*, and hanker for a place that is anything, save home? Ghalib was eloquent while saying, "I long to live in utter loneliness. With none to speak to, none to share my thoughts. In a sheer dwelling without walls and roofs. Of neighbours guarding against fate and thieves. With none to tend me if I'm sick and prostrate. And none to mourn me if I pass away".

Maybe the harsh vicissitudes of life forced him to say so. But then, he can afford it because he was a poet; a sagged soul caught up in the whirlwind of whimsy imagination, abandoning the substantial realities quite casually.

For a lay person, home remains to be the better place of living and dying. The place you eventually return to when outside world gives you dingbats. The place most suitable when life wobbles. The place where you sob on your own shoulder and nobody objects. The place where little trifles lend a colour to your persona, the one that incessantly gets de-colourized by huge travails without. The place where the heart truly is. The resort of everything—of love, joy, sorrow and sadness, mingling into bliss.

There is a delightful story of an orphan, who was being cared for in a Children's Hospital. Each night the kind nurse tucked him into bed and said-'I love you'. The little kid did not respond and often looked quite blank when she uttered these words. Once he somehow uttered-'Sister, what does love mean?' The nurse realized his innocent predicament. She picked him up, hugged and patted him, and gave a kiss, saying—'that's love'. As she put him back into bed, he beamed up at her and said-'I like it'.

Love is one of the great gifts that God has given to humans. It is one of those mysterious things that happen between people. Naturally, one of the great expressions of love is to be found in the marriage. However, very sadly, this happy relationship seems under attack at present, and one in three marriages break up constantly.

A successful marriage has a direct bearing on a happy home life. It is within the marriage sphere that true love blossoms, and it is guarded and cherished as well. This in spite of a ridiculous fad warning people not to marry just because they were in love! It is not easier to find complete fulfillment outside marriage even for those who love each other. True love is unselfish, for it helps us see how we can make our partner happy rather than just thinking how he/she can make us happy. And that's why home is the place where relationships are learned and framed. It is the place where children learn how to relate to other human beings. If the relationships are unhappy here in the early days of growth and development, then the children may find it very difficult to know how to relate to others in a society as they grow up. It does seem true that children from unhappy homes find it harder to have successful marriages than children who spend their formative years in happy homes and then marry.

Home is the ideal place to teach respect for authority. In recent surveys and studies undertaken by various social institutions over the world, it has been discovered that the third highest priority among the people was 'Law and Order'. This followed 'Good Health' and 'Family Life'. This concern arises out of the fact that there seems to have been a breakdown in respect for authority and law at the moment. One reason could well be in the breakdown of so many marriages and the failure of parents to teach their children basic values of life, including respect for others. If a child does not learn respect for others at an early age, it is unlikely that he will acquire it later.

Home is the place where children learn the most about life and the way to act. It is astonishing how receptive they are by the time they are three. Many feel that the character is well formed by the time a child is seven. Hence the importance of a happy home environment in which the child can develop. And happy home inevitably is linked with a happy marriage.

Media often portrays the problems of marriage. It seems to project the tension, break-up, and the infidelity in marriages rather than the beauty and true love that can and should be found. It seems that sordid tales and bizarre revelations make for much better viewing figures than the portrayal of the ideal. Thus, it is easy for many young people to come to conclusion that the 'distorted and unhappy' are actually the norms for marriage.

What we all, perhaps, tend to ignore is the fact that even in the best of marriages, conflicts and tensions do arise. What makes a *strong marriage* is the way that these are dealt with. The need is of listening in depth. Everyone seems so busy that they do not have time to communicate or even know how to. Many of them do not listen to what their partner is *really* saying. It is possible that a wife may be complaining to her husband that he does not take her for outing or buy her little surprises. This may hurt him. But, in reality, she may be expressing her anxiety about the feeling that she is no more appealing to him as she was once. She is, therefore, simply seeking reassurance.

Such subtlety in communication needs to be unraveled and understood. In it you can find out what makes your partner happy, what he/she expects of you, and what role each of you wish to have in the marriage. It is so much more positive to express appreciation rather than criticism, and true bonds can be nurtured only when the whole family expresses love often in word and deed.

Tensions can come into marriage often because the partners are not sure of the role they play. It used to be that the man went out and earned, and the woman stayed at home, managing the household. However, the roles have changed. Today, it may be that the wife is a much better financier or gardener than the husband, and thus takes over this job. It could be that the husband really enjoys cooking or housework and wishes to do more of it. As long as you know what part you want to play and have discussed it, and are happy, then there is no reason why men and women cannot accommodate a little flexibility in their commonly accepted roles, and be happy without any hassles.

Why to allow minor differences to be dragged on and on? Life is too small to be little, and too beautiful to be spoiled by trifles. It has its Sabbaths and Jubilees in which the world appears as a hymeneal feast, and home as a small magic world, a mystic circle that surrounds comforts and virtues never known beyond its hallowed limits...

'Mid pleasures and places, although we may roam. Be it ever so humble, there's no place like home'.